BUILDING REALISTIC MODEL RAILROAD
SCENERY

Kathy Millatt

On the cover: A New York, New Haven & Hartford RR Budd RDC enters the scene on Kathy Millatt's HO scale New England model railroad.

Back cover, from left: Kathy shows how to create rutted country lanes, and how to build model trees from florists wire.

Firecrown Media
605 Chestnut St., Suite 800
Chattanooga, TN 37450
www.Shop.Trains.com

© 2022 Kathy Millatt
All rights reserved. This book may not be reproduced in part or in whole by any means whether electronic or otherwise without written permission of the publisher except for brief excerpts for review.

Published in 2022
28 27 26 25 24   3 4 5 6 7

Manufactured in China

ISBN: 978-1-62700-876-1
EISBN: 978-1-62700-877-8

Editor: Eric White
Book Design: Kelly Katlaps/Lisa Schroeder

Library of Congress Control Number: 2021940977

Introduction

When I was asked to write this book, I was delighted to be able to share so many techniques I have learned over the years. Realistic scenery is achievable by everyone, whether you are modeling a small 4 x 8-foot layout or a massive basement empire. I love experimenting and have tried all these techniques, either on small test dioramas or on my own layouts. For me the ultimate compliment is when a photo of my models is mistaken for the real thing.

Modeling realistic scenery is a journey, and some of you reading this book will be complete beginners. There are basic techniques from gluing to painting throughout this book that will get you started on your own scenery. As you advance, there are many more skills and techniques you can add to your arsenal, and these are also covered. I hope you will find both knowledge and inspiration throughout this book.

Realistic scenery is not just a bunch of techniques to learn though; it is also about observation and planning. I cannot recommend enough that you obtain a wide range of photos of the area you are modeling, or that you visit in person and spend an afternoon just looking at the colors, textures and level of detail, not just in the scenery, but the buildings, roads and railroads. Armed with that, you can flick through this book and see just which techniques or methods will suit your scene.

Most of all, I hope this book will enable you to bring your own scenery to life.

Contents

Chapter 1 Planning
Every project starts with a good plan 6

Chapter 2 Basic tools and materials
We all love buying kits but what do you really need? 22

Chapter 3 Firm foundations
Fantastic scenery needs firm foundations 31

Chapter 4 Track
The main scenic model on every layout is its trackwork 39

Chapter 5 Backdrops
Backdrops help free our layouts from the confines of our
basements or the edges of our dioramas 47

Chapter 6 Rocks and stones
Whether you buy them, cast them, or carve them,
you're likely to need bare rocks 68

Chapter 7 Earth, gravel, and mud
Scenery starts from the ground up 80

Chapter 8 Roads and paths
Wherever there are people, there will need to be roads
and paths running seamlessly through the layout 88

Chapter 9 Trees, bushes, and grass
Options abound for modeling almost any place on Earth 107

Chapter 10 Water
Whether you want a puddle or an ocean, these
techniques will help you achieve your goals 157

Chapter 11 Buildings
Railroads need a purpose and buildings provide not
only scenery but also a reason for railroad operations 179

Chapter 12 Details
The details we add set the scene and bring your layout to life .. 186

CHAPTER ONE

Planning

I make no apologies that this is one of the longest chapters in the book because the concepts and planning are key to realistic scenery. I was recently contacted by an experienced modeler who builds stunning models, often on separate dioramas, but overall, he was unhappy with his layout and he could not quite work out why. We chatted and he shared photos and videos and it became clear that each piece of modeling was superb, but overall his layout lacked cohesiveness and was visually cluttered. Following our discussions, he found a way forward and with a few tweaks was able to overcome the issues.

Good scenery includes not just railroads but also structures, grass, bushes and trees with effective backdrops and a sense of depth beyond the few inches we have to model in. Good planning can help maximize the scenery potential. Rob Thoms skillfully shows all these elements on his HO scale Boston & Maine Railroad. *Rob Thoms*

It is important to have a vision of what you want to achieve, whether it be track plans, era, location, time of day, or weather. Without this vision, your layout can lack realism across the whole area. Once you have the concept of what you want your layout to look like, you can start to plan the scenery.

Where to start?

Some people love planning and others love to jump right in, but a basic scenery plan drawn up before you begin will help. It is important to know what you want to achieve, whether it will fit in the available space, what tools and materials you will need, and what skills and techniques you will need to master to show off your layout to its best. My layouts used to start with the track plan and I would fit the scenery around it. However, with a little more thought in the planning stages, I can ensure key buildings fit, leave enough room for scenic transitions, and consider what entire scenes will look like as well as whether they will fit with the scenes next to them. I find a plan also helps me to build scenery in the right order so I do not damage existing work when adding new layers.

While you are designing your track plan, you should also list the key scenery features, areas of interest and details you want to include. I keep albums of photos of items I want to model, whether that be a building or a dock front, an interesting rock face or a close-up of manhole covers. I love the research phase, so my computer is full of photos I have taken, found online and in articles or books, of every detail of the area I am modeling. This is especially important if it is not your local area. I thought I knew what New England looked like as I live in England, but when I first visited in person I came home with the thought "I need more trees!" and ripped my existing layout out to incorporate the new scenery.

While you are looking at photos, if you are considering a photo backdrop then keep an eye out for good photos you can use. Good reference photos of generic features such as sky, roads, or grass are also invaluable.

COMPOSITION INSPIRATION A model railroad can be a piece of art. When I started modeling, I was heavily influenced by a January 1989 John Armstrong article on using fine art concepts; it introduced me to the world of composition in model railroads. In today's world, our layouts are not just viewed by people who see the layout physically but also by those that see it through our photos and videos, so we need to consider all these different media and their varying requirements. *John Armstrong*

Once you have a comprehensive list, consider the shape of your scenery: Is your area flat or mountainous? The scenic contours of your location will have a huge impact on how you approach your basic scenery layers. Flat areas can be a sheet of plywood or foam, but mountains require a different approach.

If you are modeling a real location, then maps can give a useful idea of how roads, contours and other geographic features sit together. In the U.K., you can find historic (over 50 years old) Ordnance Survey maps online, which I used to plan a micro layout based on a village in Wales. In the U.S., the Sanborn Fire Insurance Maps as well as the Historic American Buildings and Engineering Surveys found online at the Library of Congress are useful for cities and towns. United States Geological Survey maps are also available online. Many libraries have similar collections, often online, and Google or Bing maps can provide further information on how scenery looks today. Although buildings and vegetation may change, the underlying scenic contours generally do not.

One key decision to nail in the planning phase is the location of buildings, roads and water; these will need flat, firm bases. Hills and mountains, waterfalls and weirs also need to be planned in as they add height to a layout. Once you have all the ideas listed, you can move onto fitting them all together and, for that, some basics of composition will help.

Composition

When planning scenery, I think in terms of scenes. These are areas of cohesive interest, such as a city block, a small wood, or a dockside. I then think of my scenes in terms of the foreground, midground and background. The foreground is brighter and has a wider variety of colors, defined leaves on trees, more details, and weathering and will draw the viewer in. This is the location to show off the best of your modeling. In shallow scenes, all the modeling may be considered foreground.

The background section may simply be the backdrop. However, this area can extend forward a few inches. Generally, I like this background section to be less detailed with muted colors and more generic vegetation. Buildings and trees can be smaller, using scaled down versions if desired. It certainly pays to not clutter the background so it does not draw attention from the detailed foreground.

Deeper layout sections have room for a midground, which is somewhere between the two and acts as a transition. You can still see tree trunks but the forms are more indistinct. This forces perspective so that the scene feels deeper than it really is, which is vital in the shallow depths of our layouts that we use to portray miles in reality.

I find that by having detail at the front of a layout, people concentrate on that and presume that the rest of the layout is as detailed. I also like to consider what the first thing is a visitor sees when they enter the layout room. It is good to have your best modeling and a really great scene up front to set the tone of the layout.

Composition helps us plan our layouts to best effect and it can make scenes seem bigger, which is important in our space-constrained layouts. There are a number of rules or theories we can use to help. As with all modeling, the art of composition can take some time to learn, and there is no one right answer. I do recommend checking frequently and changing composition if it is not working or you can see a better way.

The science of composition

There are many theories we can lift from composition for art or photography to apply to our layouts. The first point to note is how we view a scene. A person will generally view an area with rapid eye movements in short durations of only a couple of seconds, fixing on individual elements before moving on. They get the basic gist of a scene and will categorize it according to what they already know a similar scene should look like. At this point they will also skip many elements as people have a fairly narrow field of vision and the brain is trying to pull together a much wider picture of what is in front of us. By the end of this stage, they will have an idea of the major elements and basic shapes.

Then they will come back for a more detailed appraisal, taking longer to look at each item with smaller eye movements. It is at this point that they fill in the details before moving on as their attention is grabbed by something else. People in the West generally look from left to right as this is how they have been taught to read. Cars traveling from right to left have more of a chance of grabbing attention as they go against this flow. This also means that a person's focus will end up on the right hand side of a scene and give it more visual weight.

Two people will see different things in a scene depending on what interests them. A modeler's eye may be drawn to a stunning example of peeling paint, whereas their non-modeling companion may appreciate the flowers in a nearby pot.

Knowing this, we can direct where we want someone to look. Areas of high contrast or movement will attract

DEPTH OF DETAIL This scene on Brooks Stover's Buffalo Creek and Gauley Railroad perfectly captures how a less-detailed background section allows the detail in the foreground to become the focus. The foreground has a variety of textures and includes people and a high level of detailing. The background trees by contrast are little more than polyfiber covered with ground foam. *Brooks Stover*

a viewer and so should therefore be near the front of your layout. For example, a bright color such as a yellow taxi on a gray street will be seen first. If we place brighter colors at the start of the scene, they will draw attention and then we can use colors to highlight areas to be viewed.

Space

A major consideration when planning your layout is space. Most modelers want to fit as much as possible into their layouts, and I am no exception. However, if we want to highlight an object, we often place it on its own. For example, hanging one picture on a wall as opposed to placing it in the middle of a whole wall full of pictures. Our layouts need to give space to items we want to emphasize too. I personally find many layouts are very busy with no place for the eye to rest, and those jewels of modeling can get lost in the crowd.

Real life has vast areas where nothing really happens. This would make a boring layout, but we can learn lessons on how to design our layouts to give the same effect in a compact space. Firstly, do not let your layout elements compete with each other for attention. Plan the view as well as individual scenes.

I find the best way to do this is with scenic dividers, which can help split scenes apart and drive the eye back to view the area you want it to for longer, allowing it to take in the detail you have so carefully modeled. The eye will then take in each scene as a separate element, which can make the layout seem bigger. Green is a restful color the eyes find pleasing, so I have a lot of greenery between scenes in my branch section.

There are so many ways to add scenic breaks and transitions between scenes but here are some suggestions:
- Bridges
- Roads
- Watercourses
- Groups of trees
- Rock faces
- Fences
- Hills
- Tracks

ELEVATION AND APPARENT SPACE If you raise scenery toward the back of the layout, the scene appears larger as there is more surface visible; conversely if you drop your scenery down it can seem smaller as the scenery is foreshortened. Pelle Søeborg's layout includes a road that dips down, then back up and you can see that on the left of the road the scenery is clearly visible and appears quite expansive as it rises to the track level. On the right hand side, especially around the bend sign, the foreshortening effect means that the clumps of greenery merge into each other and the apparent area that is modeled is visually much smaller. *Pelle Søeborg*

PARALLEL I try not to place tracks, roads or buildings parallel to the layout edge, although often it is a necessity due to the track plan. This photo of Randy Laframboise's and Mark Sparks' layout shows that a simple straight track can be more interesting if viewed at an angle. *Randy Laframboise*

DISAPPEARING TRAIN This layout by Lee Marsh shows great composition with a rolling S-curve adding interest and increasing the apparent length of the train as the rear is not visible. Lee runs prototypical-length passenger trains, but the same technique can be used for those with shorter trains. *Lee Marsh*

COMPOSITION CONSIDERATIONS

FORE MID BACK This photo shows how a tree changes visually as it moves farther away from the viewpoint. In the foreground, you can see individual leaves, on taller trees you will see trunks and the greens are brighter. By the midground, there are still a few trunks visible on the trees at the edge of the wood, but you cannot see individual leaves and the greens are noticeably more muted. By the background, the trees are lighter and bluer in tone and individual trunks cannot be seen. Leaves are not visible and branch structure is indistinct. It is the overall shape of the tree that is visible.

SYMMETRY & BALANCE One key concept in composition is balance. This is not the same as symmetry where two equal objects are arranged as in the left hand image. Western art has a lot of symmetry whereas Eastern art is often asymmetric. Symmetry often looks artificial as nature is rarely symmetrical, but a balanced composition will be the most pleasing. Balance means that each element of a scene has equal weight, an example is one large tree balanced by a number of smaller ones. What this means in practice is that a large number of small items can overpower a much larger one, but conversely one small item can focus attention where a cluttered larger item does not. In these two photos, you can see symmetry on the left and asymmetry or balance on the right. The right hand photo works because the three smaller but brighter trees balance out the darker larger one.

 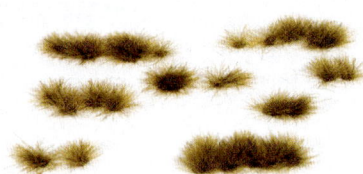

ODD-VS.-EVEN An odd number of items is more pleasing to the eye than an even number. It is also hard to create random effects as we tend to spread items more evenly than we should. For example, to place random rocks in a meadow, it is best to throw a handful on and leave them where they fall rather than arranging them. Grass tufts are the same. In these two photos, you can see that the odd numbered static grass clumps on the left look more interesting than the even numbered clumps, and also look more natural as they tend not to form straight lines.

RULE OF THIRDS This is commonly used in photography and involves dividing an image into thirds both horizontally and vertically and placing interesting objects on those lines. It is supposed to add energy and dynamism to a picture. As photography has become so commonplace, many people see our layouts first through photos.

Moving the locomotive to the right hand line gives it space to move into the scene rather than already being half way out. On a practical modeling note, place important items on the intersection of thirds in a scene and ensure there is enough space around your favorite elements to take well-composed photos. If the scene at right was a model and there was a building blocking view on the left hand side, then you may have a less pleasing photo.

CENTERED

S-CURVES S-curves will also give the eye farther to travel, allowing it to take longer and thus making the layout seem bigger. This does not just apply to track as this S-shaped creek by Lance Mindheim shows. *Lance Mindheim*

DARK AND LIGHT Thoughtful use of lighting can draw attention to scenes of interest, in dusk or dawn scenes as well as at night. In this scene, the crane and boat lighting draw you in and highlight the loading area. *Greg Shinnie*

COLOR CONTRASTS If we use a little bit of Photoshop magic to remove the yellow color from the taxis in this view of New York from the High Line, then we can see what a difference color makes in attracting attention. The left-hand image allows the eye to wander around, and the red umbrellas are the most striking part of the photo. The right-hand image directs the viewer to the taxis because of their bright color.

MIDDLE OF THE GRID

OFF CENTER

ON THE GRID LINE

COMPOSITION CONSIDERATIONS

COLOR DRAWS ATTENTION
The brighter vehicles in the foreground plus bright red doors on the near building focus the eye on that scene before the buildings behind are taken in on Arnie Hall's layout. *Lou Sassi*

FOLLOW THE LINES We can channel our viewer's attention using the technique of leading lines, that is, strong structural lines that run through a scene. Railroad tracks, roads, telegraph poles, waterways, and fences are all examples that can lead the eye through a scene and take it to the area we want to focus on. We do need to be careful the same lines do not drag our viewers out of a scene. Track can be especially guilty of doing this as it is such a strong leading line. City layouts have so many leading lines with strong horizontals and verticals that can lead your eye back and forth across a scene. Doug Kirkpatrick's layout is a great example of this with the elevated track, canopy and train taking your eye to the right, the small brick building acting as a view stop then sends your eye back around to the left with strong sweeping horizontal lines in the background buildings. The chimney can act as a point your eye stops and falls back down to the locomotive. *Paul J. Dolkos*

SCENIC BREAKS Glyn Thomas modelled late autumn/early winter with his HO scale layout based on the Central Railroad of New Jersey in Pennsylvania's Lehigh Valley. By November, the trees are bare in the foreground with a touch of autumnal color left on the backdrop hills. Tranquil scenes like this give the eye a chance to rest and increase the impact of areas of interest. *Glyn Thomas*

BREATHING ROOM Lance Mindheim is a strong advocate of leaving space and not over-compressing scenes. His ultra-realistic layouts use this philosophy in their planning approach. Lance's book, *How to Design a Model Railroad*, offers more detail. *Lance Mindheim*

Colors

I like to plan a color palette for my layout. This might sound excessive, but at the simplest level, it is a list of key products and paints I will be using, such as a certain brand of ground foam that will be the backbone color for most of my trees, or a grout color I will use for my earth color, which flows through to the paint I use to match the earth color and even to the weathering on my rolling stock.

I use my photo collections to look more deeply at the color of plants, skies, buildings, signs, rock formations, and a myriad of other details. I find that my memory is easily fooled and when I pick a color out to use, I often pick something that just does not look the same as real life.

Once you have a color palette, then you can convert it to Pantone colors or print it out and have it scanned at a DIY store to buy color-matched paints for your sky, earth, or backdrops. Color and design are key to a realistic scene.

Forced perspective

This is a useful tool to give a feeling of depth in small space. Simply put, objects get smaller and less detailed as they get farther away.

There are some extremely clever dioramas that play with perspective to show how distorting lines away from the traditional square can fool the eye. However, these require fixed viewpoints to work, so it is much easier for us as modelers to shrink the scale of objects as they get farther away. Traditionally, this has meant using N-scale or Z-scale buildings and smaller trees toward the back, but with the advent of so many computer-aided models, it is now easier to use scales in between to add a more gradual or less harsh feeling of depth. Card models can be printed at any size, for example 80 percent of our modeling scale. We will look a this more in the backdrops chapter.

My Maine seaport mock-up (page 19) shows how a 3D backdrop can be used to add depth in just a few inches. All of these strategies need to be planned before the layout scenery is built. Even subtle changes, such as smaller trees or kit buildings at the back with large ones at the front, can help sell the illusion.

Setting the scene

Before we finish the planning section, it is also worth considering a few other key factors in our scenery. There are four seasons, although many of us choose to model the summer. Over the years, I have seen beautiful autumn foliage or winter scenes on layouts. The seasons will vary by region and some seasons may even be missing in some parts of the world. Seasonal transitions can also be very interesting, such as the end of winter or the first blush of autumn.

Setting your layout in a different season can add interest or perhaps enable a key scene you want to model. You can change the season with an airbrush and paint as well

REMOVABLE-DIORAMA I have more structure kits than I can ever build and more than will fit on my layout, so I have planned for removable diorama sections. This will enable me to build all those kits easily as dioramas on my workbench, then slot them into my layout. This half complete diorama is an example. A river runs in from the left, and the water surface has been planned to join at a weir where the transition will be less visible. I have three potential dioramas for this one spot alone. This scene, though, has green space and rivers or roads to either side allowing the detail to breathe and be relished before moving on.

COLOR FADES WITH DISTANCE We will look at this more in the backdrops chapter, however, when looking at photos and considering colors for your layout, use mid-distance colors as these are the distance a typical viewer sees your layout. For example, a 2-foot viewing distance is 174 feet in HO scale. In this example you can see that the green becomes much paler and more blue as it recedes down the railroad into the distance. It might be tempting to use the bright foreground green but your layout scenery may look more realistic toned down to the middle green.

COLOR PALETTE It can help to pick a color palette for your layout if you want to set a certain tone. These are two of my layouts and the colors tell completely different stories. The left row is from my New Haven layout set on a July sunny day. The right row is from my Port Dinorwic layout, which is a dreary Welsh slate dock. The colors are a lot more muted and monotone than those of the brighter sunny layout.

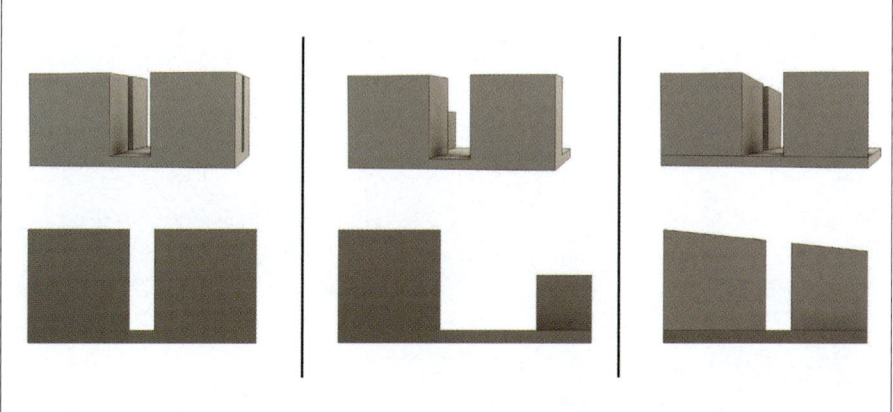

FORCED PERSPECTIVE Here are three 3D design mockups demonstrating forced perspective. The top tier photos are the expected viewpoint; the second tier are a side view. The first mockup is just four blocks evenly spaced as would happen on a layout if we use identical plastic kit buildings. Some degree of perspective will happen as we look at the buildings, but they all appear fairly similar to the viewer. The second is using an N scale building behind an HO scale building. Ideally, there would be a lot more distance to complete this illusion, as well as scenery in between, but the N-scale building does appear farther away if the distance is right. The third shows completely forced perspective with no line square other than the verticals. This requires set viewpoints to work well or the illusion is destroyed. It is best used in a controlled space such as a diorama or a view down a street where side angles cannot be seen and requires completely scratch built buildings.

4 SEASONS OAK The four season oak tree on page 16 models a quarter of the tree in each season. This is a wire armature tree with polyfiber for the canopy on the leafy seasons. Noch leaves and some airbrushing created the colors I needed.

GRAY SKIES Another factor is the weather. My first layout had a gray sky and I loved the atmosphere it gave in photos. Even on a sunny day, we can often see the aftereffects of rain with light and dark patches on the ground as it dries out, and especially around puddles on tarmac.

MORNING I love the feeling of tranquillity in Troels Kirk's early morning scene on his Coast Line Railroad. The hand-painted sky shows the first glimmer of the sun across Cranberry Wharf as the morning train arrives. *Troels Kirk*

EVENING At the other end of Troels' layout, the sky moves to evening. The first blush of a sunset is there but it is not overdone. Troels is an artist and every part of his layout reflects his tremendous talent. For the less artistic among us, a photo backdrop could be used. *Troels Kirk*

NIGHT SCENES The sun is not up yet on Thom Radice's Western & Atlantic layout. It does not take many lights to make a believable early morning scene. If night scenes are to be a feature of your layout then the lighting will need to be planned in before scenery construction starts. *Andy Salcius*

SMALL MOCKUP This mockup was created by Nigel Bowyer for a logging layout with simple card shapes and cocktail stick trees. At 9" long, it shows that mockups do not need to be large to be effective.

UTAH DESERT When we pick the railroad we model, we often pick the region too. Some railroads span vast distances allowing a wide range of choice, but others are just in one locale. Often within a region you still have the choice of urban or rural. Realistic scenery will reflect the local differences that allow a viewer to understand where your layout is set as soon as they see it. For example, this Utah desert scene by Kim Nipkow has the signature red rocks that typify that region. They are modeled using a foam base with mortar plaster spread over the top and carved while the plaster was still soft. The coloring is also typical of the area as are the scrubby bushes. *Kim Nipkow*

as completely modeling the scene from scratch. Most of the seasons with leaves can be modeled with the techniques shown in the vegetation chapter with just tweaks to the colors and leaf density.

Gray skies can be dramatic or just that average day where the sun could not be bothered to come out. To pull this off, shadows need to be muted so layout lighting should be as soft as possible. A fog machine could add to the ambience.

Early morning or sunset scenes have always been a favorite of mine, but nighttime scenes are also achievable with a bit of planning. The key thing with a sunrise or sunset scene is to ensure that the lights, and hence shadows, come from the side. When taking photographs, this can be done with extra directional lights.

Mockups

Moving on from a list to visualizing the scenery in 3D helps plan the overall impression of the layout. Mockups are a great way to do this. Build a few buildings or make mockups of them and move them around for effect. Raise them up and lower them to see what impact the height has; change the angle and perhaps change the size. Come back a week later and see if you are still happy with your mockup. Taking photos of the mockup can also help give you a different viewpoint and decide whether the scene will have good camera angles.

Practical considerations

This chapter discusses composition, color choice and many other scenery-related issues to be considered, but besides these there are the practical

FULL-SIZED MOCKUP I created this full-size mockup for a planned Maine seaport micro layout. The concept includes a 3D backdrop with forced perspective and was made in a day from card, foam core, paper towels, and a full-size track plan designed in track-planning software. The mockup taught me that the layout was too large for the space I have available, and even though I have not built the layout yet, it was an invaluable and fun exercise.

GOING DIGITAL

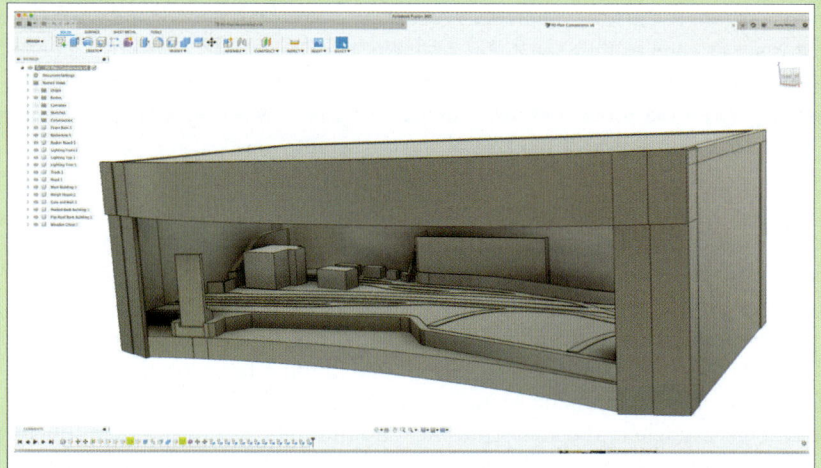

3D RENDERING Creating a mockup in a CAD program was a great help in planning how this micro layout would fit together, and I was able to work out view blockers, sight lines and scenery contours.

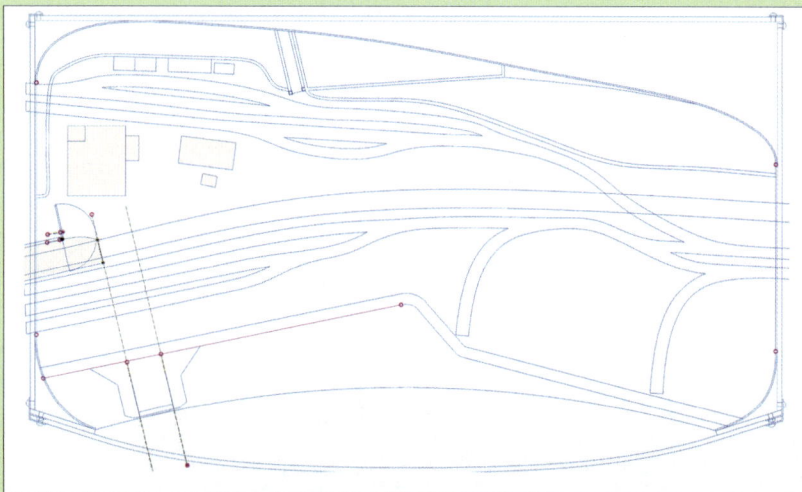

FROM PLAN TO REALITY I printed the 3D mockup plan full size when I started to build my layout, safe in the knowledge that everything would fit in place. When it came to scratchbuilding the structures, I already had the key dimensions. I had an unusual curved backdrop and I also used the design to produce 3D printed components to support the backdrop.

considerations. Room shape and size come into the track plan stage, but as far as scenery is concerned, access to reach deep areas, especially the backdrop, wiring for lighting or animations, benchwork locations for scenic features or animations, and building scenery in the easiest order for you are all vital to consider.

Order
This book is laid out in the order that I complete scenery, but many of the jobs associated with a chapter's themes will overlap with others. For example, I find it easier to do a base layer of earth, maybe a little vegetation, then pour my resin water. I find if I leave it to later, then it wicks through vegetation and other scenery and can ruin it. Unless I am doing a bog area, I prefer to pour and protect the resin early in the scenery process before doing the final ripples and finishing as almost the last task in an area.

In many layouts, the backdrop and background scenery become harder and harder to reach as more of the layout is finished. You can change your mind later, but starting at the back and working forward is a good rule of thumb.

Record keeping
Once you have finished planning, it helps to keep a record of the colors and materials used in case you need to repair or extend areas. My blog is ideal for this, but a notebook will more than suffice. I keep a record of all the materials used plus the paint colors. I also like to take a series of photos so I can check progress and how scenes are progressing, and also to remind myself how I built areas.

Planning for maintenance
It may seem odd to think about maintenance before you have even started the scenery, but some thought now can save issues later on. There are two main issues with aging scenery: dust build-up and fading. Battling dust is an inevitability and is made an uphill battle if scenery work is continuing elsewhere in the room.

The benefits of a temperature-controlled room, properly lined and fitted out with sealed floors, are immeasurable. Not all of us can afford this, but even a simple coat of paint on a concrete floor can help control dust from that source while a fitted ceiling will prevent dust from above. I have seen all sorts of systems in the railroad press over the years, from positive air pressure pushing dusty air out, to filter systems, but they are beyond most of us. Finishing a room is achievable though, and I would encourage layout owners to do so.

As an alternative, enclosing the layout can cut down the dust reaching it. Consider adding a top enclosure where no room ceiling is possible. Plastic sheeting through to permanent curtains are all options to seal the front. Dioramas are easily stored with either plastic sheeting over the top or in a box.

I build all my messy scenery in a different room if I possibly can to cut down on dust. Aerosol cans put out

REVITALIZING Even the best protected model water will get dull and dusty over time. A regular clean will help bring the shine back.

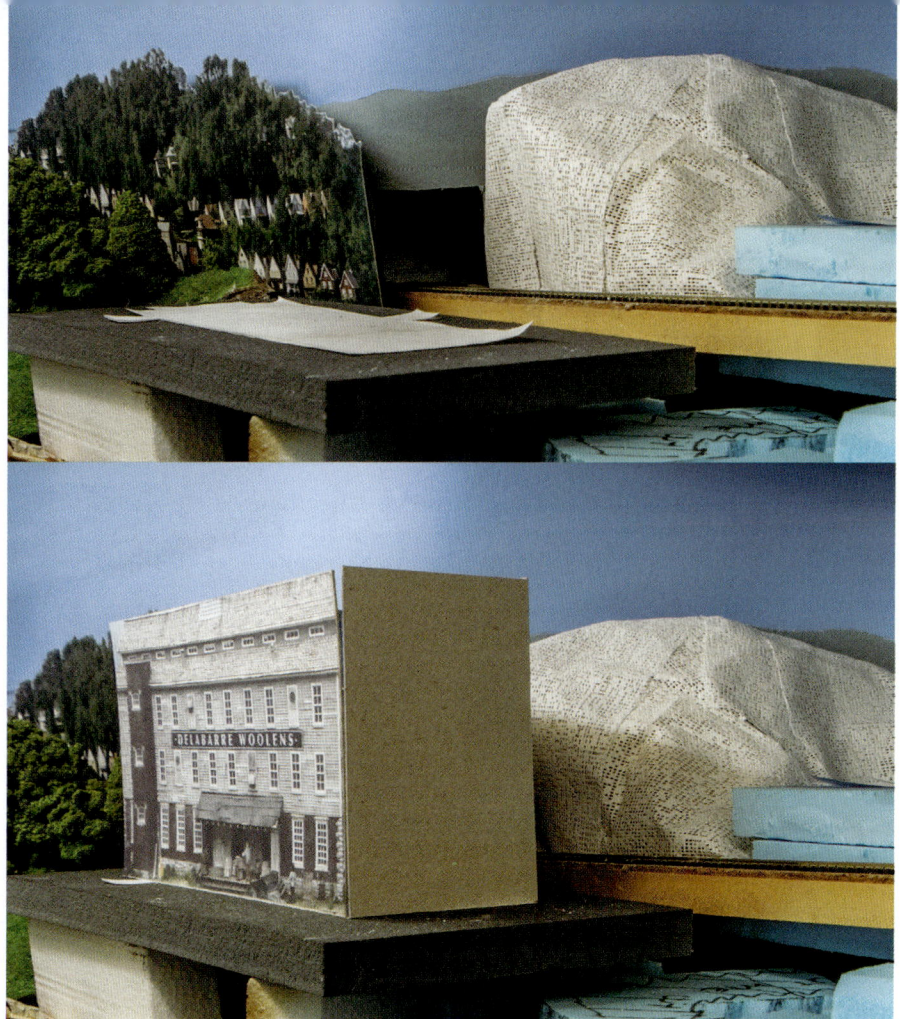

MOCKUPS DURING CONSTRUCTION Much of a layout will be defined by the track plan, but scenery can be used to complement this, including masking train entry and exit points from a layout. In the early stages of building this section of the layout, I used a mockup of a future building to see where it needed to be located to hide the end of a backdrop and where the track entered the scene.

a lot of particulates and I always try and do these outside. This may not be practicable for everyone, but using a vacuum to catch dust as it is created will help.

While considering ceilings, it is also a good time to sort out the layout lighting.

The second key issue is fading and this is caused by ultraviolet (UV) light, either from sunlight or some types of light such as fluorescents. Installing curtains or blinds on windows and choosing low UV emitting layout lighting or adding UV shields to fluorescents will go a long way to helping. The same protective curtains used to keep dust off will also keep light out.

Final thoughts

Planning will save time in the long run as you understand what to do and when. However, it is important to adapt as you build scenery and new ideas open up. Some of my best scenes have taken many iterations before I was finally happy with the result.

I find photographs are really helpful in checking my scenery. You become accustomed to a scene and do not really "see" it. Taking a photo and flipping it horizontally can help disrupt your memory so you take a fresh look.

PLANNING TABLE

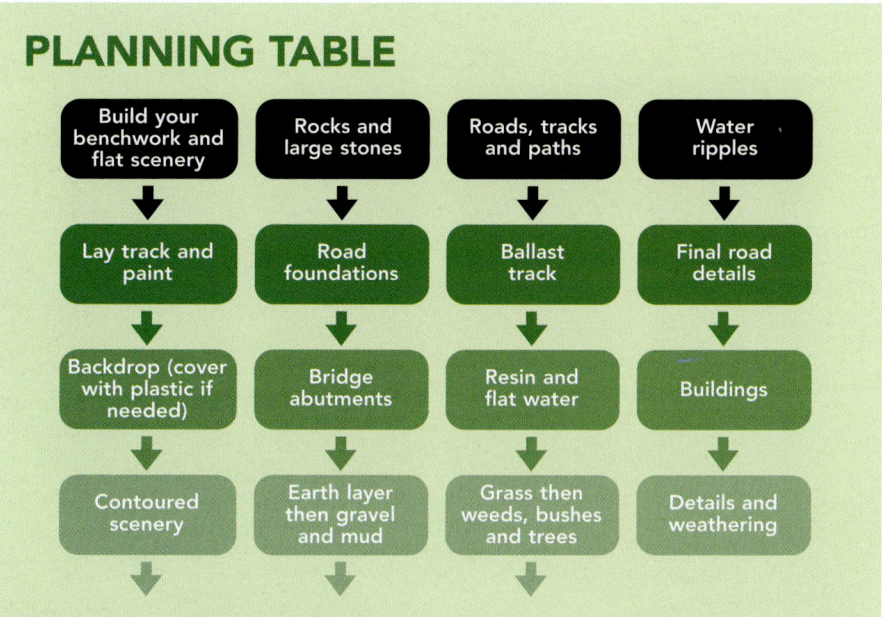

Build your benchwork and flat scenery	Rocks and large stones	Roads, tracks and paths	Water ripples
Lay track and paint	Road foundations	Ballast track	Final road details
Backdrop (cover with plastic if needed)	Bridge abutments	Resin and flat water	Buildings
Contoured scenery	Earth layer then gravel and mud	Grass then weeds, bushes and trees	Details and weathering

There is no one right way to build your scenery, but there are definitely some tasks that need doing before others or you can damage existing work or find successive jobs are harder to carry out. We will work through each step in this book.

21

CHAPTER TWO

Tools & materials

I started out with just a knife, a cutting mat, and a ruler, but then I realized tools could make my life easier. Over the years I have picked up many more tools but, while some are nice to have, you can get by with just a few basics. As you get further into the hobby and start to learn more techniques, you will need additional tools, but the vast majority do not need to be expensive and are readily available online and in hobby or do-it-yourself stores.

Weights and squares—you need these to keep items flat while glue or paint dry. I use flat-sided paving bricks for large areas and 1-2-3 machining blocks (1) or engineering squares (2) for smaller items.

Tweezers (3) and **small pliers** (4) help hold small items safely, prevent your hands from getting covered in glue or paint, and are an invaluable tool I use on almost every project.

Knives—the most important items in my basic tool kit are a couple of knives (5), a hobby knife and a box cutter/utility knife. Hobby knives with a number 11 blade are great for fine detail work, but I find a box cutter easier for large items and in the early stages of scenery. To cut safely

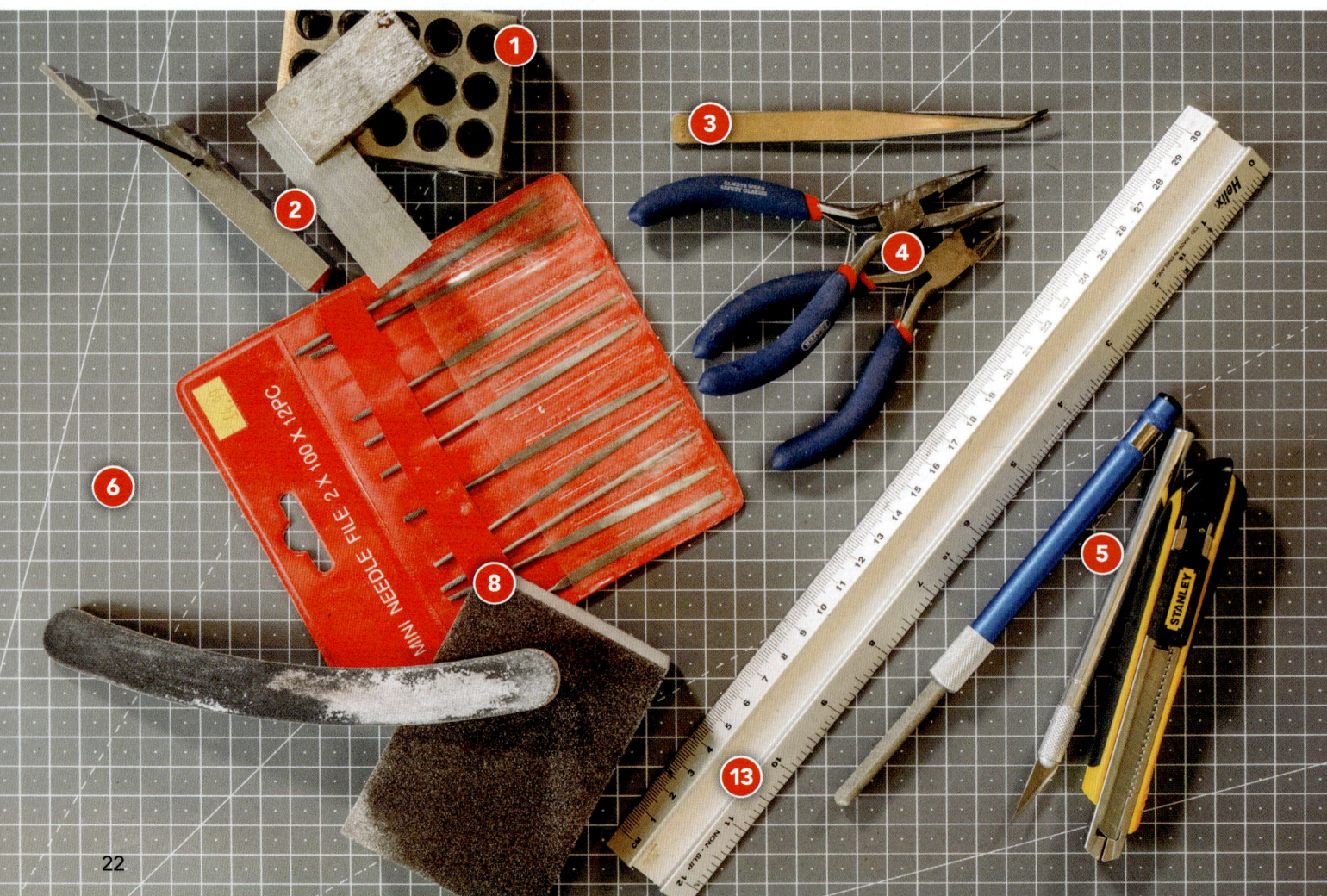

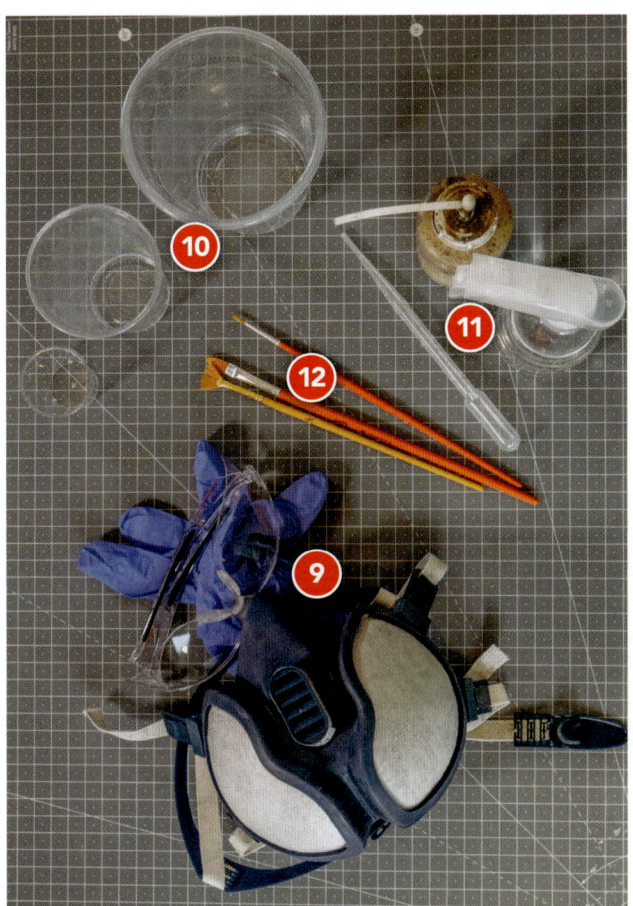

● Moving on from the Basic Tool Kit

Once you have the basics, there are items you will use more and more as time goes on and they will always find a place in my tool kit now:

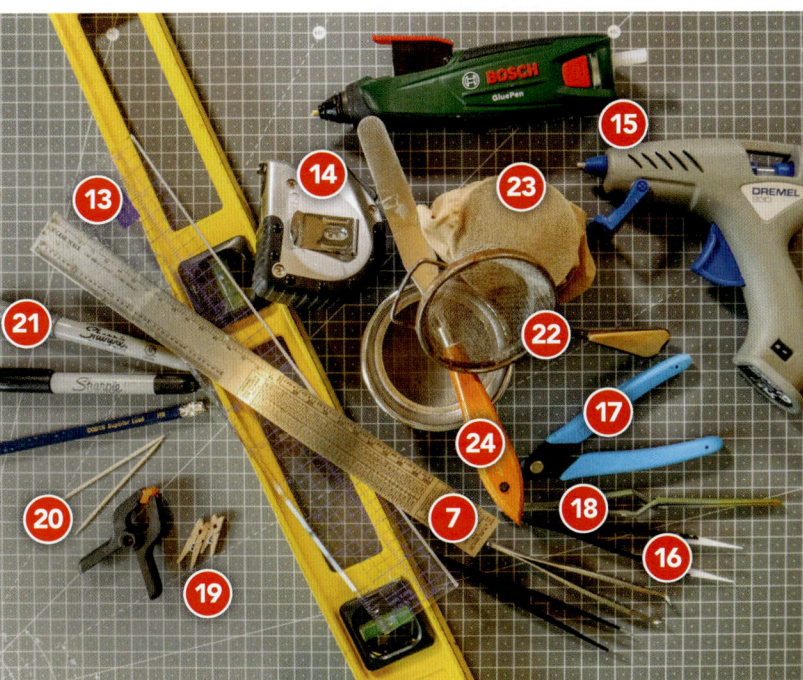

you will need to protect the surface you are cutting on, and a self-healing cutting mat (6) is ideal for this. You will also need a metal-edge ruler (7). Do not forget to buy replacement knife blades in bulk. A **knife sharpener** will also help extend the useful life of a blade.

Sanding tools from small files to emery boards and sanding blocks (8) in a range of grades will find a use in most areas of modeling.

Protective gear (9) is one of the most important items. You will need respiratory masks, gloves, and eye protectors for any spray paints or large sanding jobs. Resin dust and paint particulates are dangerous.

Disposable plastic cups and containers (10) in a range of different sizes are ideal for mixing plaster and resin, diluting glues and thinning paints.

Spray and dropper bottles (11)—scenery involves a lot of glue and these are essential to ensure even coverage and that everything is firmly attached. You can use disposable pipettes, but a dropper bottle is quicker as it holds a much larger volume. Likewise, I prefer trigger type spray bottles over pump action as they are easier on the hands if you are doing a lot of scenery in one sitting.

Paintbrushes (12) in all sizes from artists' fine detail brushes to decorators' large paint brushes for painting backdrops. I also use disposable foam brushes for some glue applications, and sponges can give a different texture application. Both of these can be washed and used many times.

Rulers (13)—there are many types of ruler, and I recently discovered clear acrylic rulers with a metal edge. Along with scale rules, which measure in the scale you are modeling, these can make cutting simpler. A good **metal tape measure** (14) will also help on larger projects as will a yardstick.

Hot glue gun (15)—this is one optional item I find myself using more and more. It is good for the early stages of scenery, and I have both wired and wireless versions. The latter do not last long but they are great for hard-to-reach spots. More tweezers in different angles and sizes are helpful, and ceramic tip tweezers (16) are good for holding hot items. **Sprue nippers** (17) are excellent for working with plastic kits and cleaning up resin 3D prints. Self-clamping tweezers (18) are useful when painting or spraying glue on small items.

Miniature clothes pegs/pins (19) are also useful. An assortment of clips, clamps, and clothes pegs will help hold everything securely while you work. Toothpicks (20) can be useful to impale items, but I also use them extensively to apply glue in small drops.

Markers—silver Sharpies (21) work well on dark materials, and a good pencil and fine black marker will help with accurate measuring and cutting.

Sieves and palette knives—spreading scenery materials can be done in so many ways, but these are top of my list. I started off using tea strainers (22) for fine tile grout, but a cheaper option is a spray paint cap covered with a pair of old tights (23). I also use a sieve that originally came with a starting snow set but is perfect for any fine material. For plaster and Sculptamold, a palette knife (24) or an old brush can help.

My phone is an invaluable tool. I use it to take progress pictures and videos, make notes, look up information or buy products. But besides those obvious actions, there are a number of helpful apps I use: spirit level, conversion—from imperial to metric (and vice versa) or from full-size to scale measurements, plus I can use it to control lighting and animations on my layouts. When all else fails, I can use it to call a friend for help.

Finally, a **dust pan and brush, paper towels, and a vacuum cleaner** will all find uses beyond just the obvious ones of cleaning. The vacuum and dust pan can be used to reclaim excess scenery materials. I use both a dedicated small hand held vacuum or just a pair of tights over the end of the big vacuum. Paper towels can do more than just mop up spills, such as becoming a tarpaulin, roofing or even a base scenery material if soaked in plaster.

● Advanced tools

There are some tools you may need for certain jobs and there are many more tools you can buy that will help with accuracy, repetition or finish. Once I have a tool, I often wonder how I modeled without it, for example, my 3D printers.

Magnifier and lights (1)—sad to say but I now find some modeling easier with a magnifier. There are some excellent modeling lamps with magnifiers or visors that can help with the small details.

Hot wire tools (2)—when you are working with foam you can use an ordinary kitchen carving knife, but some foams can also be cut with hot wire tools. These can be a worthwhile investment if this is your chosen base material.

Static grass applicators (3)—this is something we will cover in detail in Chapter 9, but a static grass applicator is a must for grass. I started with a cheap puffer bottle but soon moved on to the electric version.

Rock molds are by far the easiest way to model detailed rocks on your layout. We will look at all the methods in Chapter 6, but a range of different sized molds of appropriate strata will be beneficial.

You can make scenery out of a lot of "found" items from the garden or kitchen. Natural materials may be a little large, and a kitchen blender can reduce them to scale size. You can also make your own ground foam. I have a dedicated scenery **blender**.

Airbrushes can be useful in painting scenery, but come into their own when adding layers of weathering to a scene or painting vegetation. Their ability to add a fine haze of paint is not easy to achieve with brushes. For scenery work, an expensive airbrush is not needed, but once you have one, your rolling stock and buildings will also benefit. It is important to either ventilate properly or wear masks when spraying paint—preferably both.

A **vinyl or hobby cutting machine** can be used to cut or score styrene and wood, and can be invaluable in producing larger scale vegetation such as ferns or palm leaves. Similar tasks can be achieved with a laser cutter, but they require space, ventilation and cooling that goes beyond a basic hobby machine.

3D PRINTING

I cannot imagine modeling without a **3D printer** now. In a couple of years, they have become my number one tool. Mine run 24/7 as I print everything from people to bridges to components I could not find any other way. Sites such as Shapeways mean you do not even need to own a printer to access 3D prints.

There are two key types: filament and resin. I use my filament printer for larger or less detail-critical prints such as components or basic shells. My resin printers give fine detail prints I use for everything from people and animals to windows and rolling stock. Although the print size used to be quite small, my latest acquisition has a much larger volume, enabling me to print entire buildings in one go. 3D printers have become much more affordable in recent years. The pictured printers were less than $400 each, and give excellent results. At this price point, the filament printer needs a little tinkering to print well, and there is a learning curve. Mine is currently printing ABS and is in a homemade enclosure to prevent drafts. You will also need 3D design files to print, but these are readily available online, both free and paid, and there are numerous free CAD programs you can use to design your own prints. Just be warned, the design phase is not always quick. You may be moving your modeling time from the workbench to the computer.

 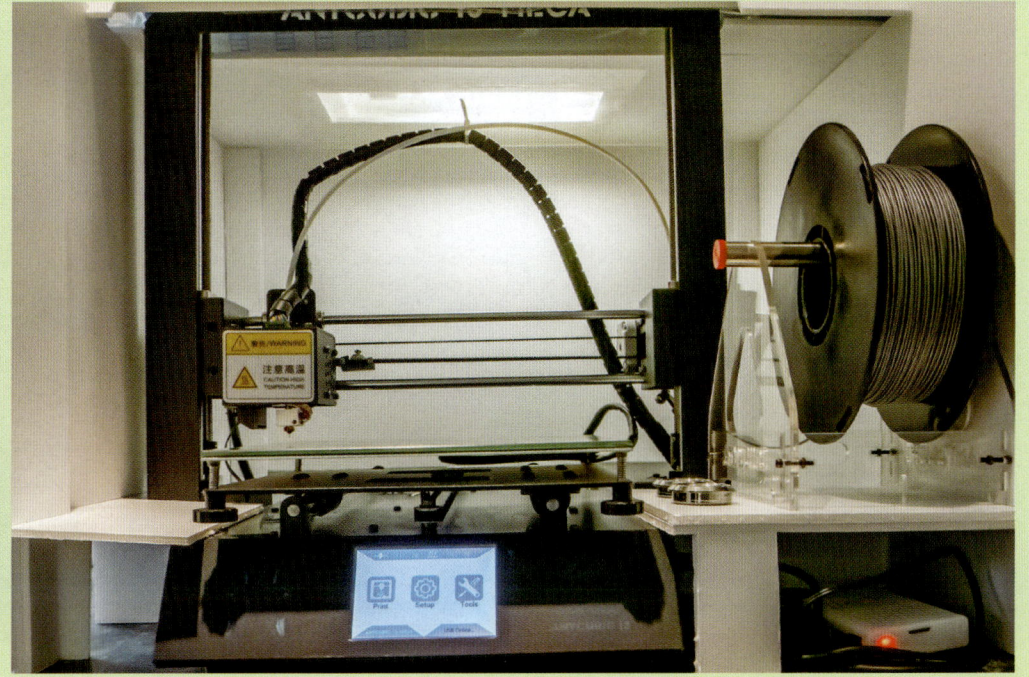

● Basic materials

Just like the scenery tools, you can start with only a few basic materials but over time, you will build up a library of different materials suited to certain tasks:

GLUE AND PAINT

GLUE AND PAINT

Wet water (1)—I use one-third 99 percent isopropyl alcohol to water to pre-wet scenery before gluing. It will break down the surface tension so the glue will sink in. Some people use a few drops of dishwashing liquid, which is much cheaper but I find isopropyl alcohol to be more effective and does not leave bubbles on the surface.

Range of glues (2)—white (PVA) glue, cyanoacrylate adhesive (super glue, both thin and gel), and hot glue are my favorites. Some tasks may be easier with specialist glues but I get by with white glue 90 percent of the time. To glue scenery, I generally use a dilute mix of either one-sixth or one-third white glue and water. I use fine spray bottles to apply the one-sixth mix because at higher concentrations they tend to clog. Any particularly large scenery items are either pre-glued with full strength glue, or I use a dropper bottle to add the stronger one-third mix. I have recently moved to using matte Mod Podge in place of white glue as it dries to a matte finish, whereas some PVAs can have a slight sheen when dry.

Paints (3)—it is useful to have large pots of your earth and sky colors. I use emulsion/latex paint for my sky and have it custom mixed to match a photo at my local DIY store. My earth color is generic raw umber I buy as an artists' acrylic color. A range of other earth and rock colors are also needed, and acrylics are the easiest to find and work with.

EARTH AND FOLIAGE

Tile grout, sand, and earth (4)—I use tile grout as my earth layer as it is easy to get, sets with very little glue as it is a cement, and comes in a wide range of suitable colors. I find unsanded grout needs one-third silver sand mixed in because otherwise the glue does not sink into the fine grout powder and either balls on the surface or leaves the lower layers unstuck. Earth from a garden or backyard is also useful, but you will need to sieve it to remove large stones and lumps, and it contains a lot of organic matter so may appear a richer color brown. Sand on its own can add a different texture to areas.

Ground foam (5)—this is exactly what it says, finely ground foam, but it comes in a range of colors from earth to green and textures from fine to coarse. I use it in all my scenery to add texture and vegetation.

Found scenery materials are everywhere (6)—from the gutters to back gardens. I have used rosemary and lavender stems as tree trunks and regularly carry a bag on a walk to pick up twigs, dead leaves and other natural detritus. The silver birch tree catkins shed spacers that are like maple leaves in larger scales. They work well in O scale or larger, and are examples of nature providing perfect modeling material.

Static grass (7)—modelers can represent grass realistically using static grass, which is made from fibers that stand upright with a static charge. You do not need an electronic static grass applicator as you can use an inexpensive nylon puffer bottle, but if you are doing large areas, you will soon want the ease of an electronic applicator.

EARTH AND FOLIAGE

● More materials

Once you have the basics, there are a vast array of materials that you can use. It is worth trying some out to see what you like. It may seem that these are long lists, but the tools are one off purchases and the materials will go a long way. I had my first bag of tile grout for over 15 years and was disappointed when I came back to repurchase and it had been discontinued because it was the perfect color and texture.

SHEET GOODS

A plentiful supply of extruded foam (8), styrene (9) and card sheets (10), both plain and embossed, plus styrene, wood and brass shapes and strips (11) in various sizes, are invaluable in scratchbuilding small elements or helping with basic construction of models from bases to buildings to bridges.

SHEET GOODS

GROUND WORKS

Sculptamold (12) —is a lightweight plaster and papier mache pulp mix that is easily mixed and makes a good base layer for scenery. It can be smoothed as it dries, and is one of my favorite products. It can be expensive to use in bulk, but there are plenty of homemade recipes on the internet.

Plaster cloth (13) —another product I use for base scenery. These are discussed in more detail in the next chapter.

Clay (14) —from air-drying to foam, as well as plaster, can be used for ground works, walls and rock faces and even roads.

GROUND WORKS

ADHESIVES

There are far more glues than the basic three and I have boxes full of bottles and tubes. Silicone adhesives (15) can be used to represent water, glue and glaze (16) can be used for windows, tacky glue (17) is a thicker white glue, epoxy (18) is good for strong bonds, office glue (19) sticks or double-sided tape (20) can help with attaching tiles and corrugated sheeting, expanding glues such as Gorilla Glue (21) can bond uneven surfaces, dry glues (22) can be used in ballast or scenery, and contact adhesives (23) make firm bonds. I use masking tape to mask off scenery, such as track, when doing messy scenery next to it or to hold items together while gluing. You can even use it as a base layer to fill a gap in the scenery. Scotch invisible tape gives a lovely clear matte finish perfect for signs. Specialist plastic glue (24) will be needed for plastic kits and the list goes on.

ADHESIVES

PAINTS

Beyond the basic earth color paints, you will need a variety of colors and types of paint for different scenery applications. Artist's acrylics (1) now come in heavy body brands with a really dense pigment mix that provide deep colors. Oil paints and water-soluble oil paints (2) are good for weathering. Gloss medium (3) or Mod Podge (4) are clear acrylic products you can use to make ripples on water. Matte and satin sealants (5) can be very helpful, as well as Dullcote, and some are now foam-safe where previously the solvents would have eaten foam away. Beyond artists supplies, I also use a lot of car spray primers in gray, red oxide, black (6), and white as the base coat for buildings or rocks. Model paints (7) come in small bottles, but a wide range of colors and finishes. Finally, there are a dizzying array of weathering products from enamel washes (8) to finely ground pigments (9) now available for modeling from many well known brands. Before this I used a hobby knife blade to scrape artists chalk pastels (10) to get a powder. I still use this for unusual colors and either use a brush to apply it dry or mix it to a slurry with isopropyl alcohol to get a matt paint that dries to a very chalky finish, which is perfect for weathering and fading.

FOREGROUND DETAILS

I use scale leaves (11) for my foreground scenery because they look more realistic. They are normally a little oversize, but the eye reads them as correct because it is expecting to see leaves on trees and bushes. Rubberized horse hair (12), polyfiber (13) and postiche (14) are all used as a base before adding leaves to bushes and trees. There are so many detail parts to choose from. Many suppliers now provide laser cut details from TV aerials to window coverings, but photo-etched brass (15), resin (16) and white metal castings and 3D printing are also options. Your local hobby store will have beads and other items you can repurpose (17). These extra layers of detail can really sell a scene and are worth adding in the foreground.

WASHES

Both enamel and oil washes are just dilute paints with a high solvent content, so they can easily be made from any paints that you already have. Oil paints are now available as water soluble, so you can even dilute those with water. I use enamel washes mostly in plastic or resin modeling where I have painted with acrylic colors. The enamel solvents will not affect the acrylic paints and so can be used in any concentration. If the base paint is enamel, using an acrylic wash can avoid any issues with disturbing the initial paint layers.

WASHES

Washes are a tool box staple. Simply, they are diluted paint or ink used to bring out detail in castings, cracks, and around raised details. They are generally used toward the end of the painting process as part of the weathering process. There are three main types:
- Isopropyl alcohol and india ink washes
- Enamel and oil washes
- Acrylic washes

They are largely interchangeable, but each have plus points and better uses.

ENAMEL WASHES

ISOPROPYL ALCOHOL WASH RECIPES

Light Wash:
1 teaspoon india ink
1 pint isopropyl alcohol 99 percent
Uses: bringing out painted details

Medium Wash:
2-2.5 teaspoons india ink
1 pint isopropyl alcohol 99 percent
Uses: weathering wood

Dark Wash:
3-4 teaspoons india ink
1 pint isopropyl alcohol 99 percent
Uses: bringing out details on rock faces, castings, etc.

ALCOHOL WASHES

I have used these mixes for over 15 years and my recipes are all shamelessly cribbed from Bob van Gelder's South River Modelworks. These have been a staple for modelers for decades because they are versatile and flow well into all the nooks and crannies. The only issue I have is with adding subsequent layers as the ink will rewet, and sometimes painting over the top can pick up some of the ink color. They are meant to be used last in the process so this is not a major issue.

Military modelers have been using dedicated enamel washes in a range of weathering colors for years. These have become more popular with model railroaders in recent years and I have racks of various shades such as Slimy Grime Light or Dark Rust. The two I use most are a neutral wash I use to add dust and earth stains, and a dark wash I use to add definition to cracks and details. These premixed bottles are handy and easy to use. The solvent is mineral spirits, which flows well. The advantage over acrylic washes is that the wash can be cleaned up with solvent once dry to remove unwanted areas or an overly heavy application. This does become harder with time, so it is best not to wait too long before tidying up the wash.

ACRYLIC WASHES

Acrylic washes have been the poor cousins of the other washes as they are less likely to flow through cracks. In recent years, they have improved and can now be bought or homemade. Scenery can absorb a lot of wash, so homemade options are much cheaper and can provide very effective results. These washes use the most family friendly solvent, water, but do not rewet, meaning it is easy to layer other glues or paints over the top without the wash coloring later layers.

Washes do not just have to be black and I find a brown wash equally as useful.

ACRYLIC WASH RECIPE

- 50ml matte medium
- 5ml flow improver or slightly less of dishwashing liquid or rinse aid
- 50ml water
- 40-100 drops acrylic ink. Black needs around 40 but brown needs around 100. It will vary depending on brand.
- Add the ingredients to a dropper bottle.
- Shake well.
- Test for strength—it may look slightly gray before it dries because of the matte medium.
- Add more ink if needed.
- Spray washes need a finer mix, so I use only 10ml matte medium to get the fine spray I want. It will depend on your spray bottle.

This recipe is for a fairly strong wash that I use on rock work, staining details, and for adding definition to scenery. I do have a slightly more dilute version that I spray for large areas of scenery.

One of the most common uses of a wash is to highlight the details on rock castings. Here I am using a black homemade acrylic wash on a rock casting.

● Basic skills

Besides buying tools and materials, you will need to learn some basic skills that may be new. These are mostly about training your eyes and hands and learning to use your imagination to work in three dimensions.

Fine control for painting and modeling does improve with practice. I notice when I have not modeled for a while, everything seems harder and it does take time to get back into it. You will need to take on some basic painting and weathering, but with the right techniques, explained in this book, they are very easy to pick up. More complex techniques, such as 3D design or electronics, can become hobbies in themselves.

The techniques in this book are not beyond a beginner, and some of the scenes shown are from my earliest work. Modeling is a continuous learning curve and one of the key takeaways is that you will improve. I recommend starting on a practice diorama or toward the back of your layout until you have learned the technique. You may need to be prepared to do an area more than once or to change it later as you improve.

STEP BY STEP • PAINTING

This is my normal four step process to paint almost everything: prime, base, wash, dry brush:

1 I always prime my plastic or resin pieces just to make sure that the subsequent layers of paint stick. I use either a basic car gray primer or Tamiya fine gray surface primer. Both are lacquer based and as they are aerosols, I try to do them outside, weather permitting.

2 I either hand-paint or airbrush a base color. This is an acrylic brown model paint.

3 I add a dark enamel wash into all the nooks and crannies.

4 Finally, once the wash is dry, I drybrush a lighter color, here a green gray acrylic model paint, over the raised areas. This works best on detailed models, but can also be used on edges of most models.

CHAPTER THREE

Firm foundations

Fantastic scenery needs firm foundations. While you do not need to be able to stand on your layout, you do want to make sure that there are no unexpected model earthquakes or sink holes.

This S scale scene uses foam and Sculptamold to create a lightweight but robust base. The rocks are plaster cast in Woodland Scenics molds.

Your landscape will guide you

Once you have your scenery plan and you have acquired some basic tools and materials, you will want to get started on building your layout. Before you do that, it is worth taking some time to consider what materials you will use to build the base layer beneath the scenery.

The first thing that needs to be built and tested is all the benchwork supporting any track. The materials you use to build this can also be used for the scenery base, but in some instances there may be better options. Trackwork itself always needs to be on a firm, even base and that is generally either a wood product or extruded-foam insulation board. It is important to get your track laid and running well before you add the majority of the scenery. The scenery process can gum up unprotected trackwork and may hide some sections of track if you have tunnels or hidden staging. If everything is working flawlessly before you start scenery, you have a better chance of it working afterward too.

For the very simplest scenery base, you can take a sheet of a wood product, such as plywood, medium-density fiberboard (MDF), or extruded-foam insulation board and just add scenery directly on top. This will give a very flat scene, which may be just what is needed. Even if your scenery is mostly flat, areas around bridges over the track will need to be built up, and some areas beneath the track height, such as river beds, may need to be cut away.

My general inclination is to put flat sheets of plywood or extruded-foam insulation board under track, structures, some tarmac areas such as roads or car parks, and also under flat water areas. I may add blocks of wood or extruded-foam insulation board under areas with heavy foreground trees to give a firm base, but I generally leave other areas as either voids to fill or easy-to-carve foam. This gives me greater latitude to create flowing scenic contours.

31

SCENERY LAYERS

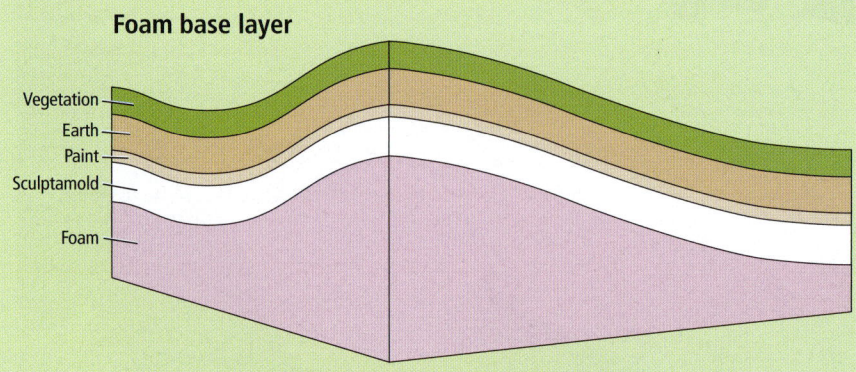

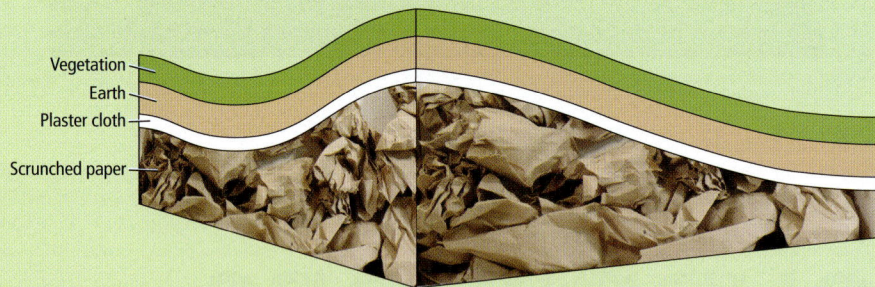

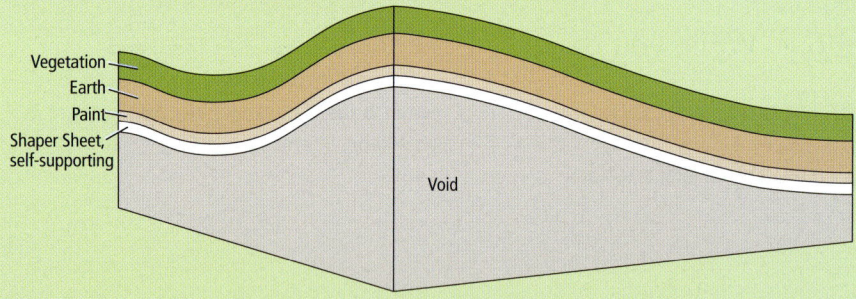

There are two types of scenery bases. The first is a solid base layer, such as extruded-foam insulation board, and the second is a hard shell type, such as plaster cloth or shaper sheet. The foundation work can even start to merge into the ground and earth scenery.

Unlike the trackwork, scenery itself does not need rock-solid foundations. But there will be a fair amount of water used in the scenery process to glue the earth and vegetation layers, so the scenery base layer does need to factor this in.

On my first layout, I did not support the end of a piece of very thin plywood used as the base of a flat scene. When I added water with the scenery process, it warped, leaving a gaping crack in the ground. I had to brace and then re-scenic the area.

There are two main types of base layer, solid or hollow, and these determine the layers needed above it. A foam base layer can be used to give all the contours needed, then the finer detail can be added with Sculptamold or any type of ground goop.

A hard shell method, such as plaster cloth, will need a lightweight support underneath to create the contours. I often use scrunched up paper, but any foam or card scraps will do. This method can use the earth layer to fill the holes in the plaster cloth or, alternatively, a thin skim of Sculptamold will do the trick. If I do use the earth layer to fill gaps, then it is thicker than normal, so I do not always paint the plaster cloth first.

Finally, Shaper Sheet, a Woodland Scenics product, is a variant of the hard shell scenery but it is self-supporting, eliminating the bottom support layer. It comprises a thick foil layer with a fleece layer glued to it. The modeler mold the sheet to shape, then a thin layer of liquid plaster is added, which sets and creates a firm base. I find it useful when modeling water as it will not leak.

OPEN AND CLOSED Relatively flat scenery can use sheets of a wood product or extruded foam. More contoured scenery only needs to be flat and level on track areas. The rest of the benchwork can be cut away or left open and a different scenery base installed.

In this construction photo by Pelle Søeborg, you can see two types of base in action. On the right hand side, with level scenery, the whole area is covered with a flat sheet, whereas on the left hand side, only the track subroadbed itself is firmly installed and scenery areas are left open. *Pelle Søeborg*

There are a vast range of potential products to suit all inclinations and pockets. Over time, you will find your favorites and this chapter will suggest some of the best options currently available.

TIP! Remember to install any tunnel portals and tunnel liners before you cover that area in scenery.

COMPLETED SCENES This shot of the finished scenery shows how Pelle treated the scenery on each side differently. The road on the right is flat and runs along at track level, whereas the road on the left moves up and down in height and adds a lot of visual interest. His scenery base options were carefully thought out to allow both types of final scenery. *Pelle Søeborg*

FOAM BASE LAYERS

OPTIONS One of my favorite products is foam. It is normally stacked in layers, glued together, then carved into shape. It is lightweight, easy to adjust later, comes in multiple thicknesses from ¼ inch to 8 inches, can be used as a track subroadbed if properly braced, and is also easily available. If you or any friends have building work done, then you may have a free supply, but otherwise it can be found in your local DIY store.

There are three main types of foam—XPS (extruded polystyrene) foam that can be carved with hot wire tools (bottom in photo), PIR (polyisocyanurate) foam (top in photo) that will need kitchen carving knives, and expanded polystyrene. I use all of them and they each have their advantages.

XPS FOAM is a slightly softer foam that can be cut with hot wire tools. These are very easy to use and create less mess than carving with a knife, although I still cut straight lines with a box cutter knife. Good ventilation is required for hot wire as the fumes are toxic. For straight cuts, score with a knife, then snap over a straight edge. You can also sand the denser varieties of this type of foam.

XPS foam is not solvent resistant and can be eaten away by some glues and paints. Hot glue, Gorilla glue, or white glue (if you allow extra time for it to dry as it needs air to set) are all suitable, but you can also buy specialist foam glues that do not require air to set. The specialist glues can sometimes be carved with hot wire tools, which can be a benefit when stacking layers of foam before carving. For large stacks of foam, and while glue is setting, it can be helpful to pin the layers together with bamboo skewers or screws.

You can just paint the foam and add scenery to it, but I would normally add another layer on top, such as Sculptamold or ground goop. This adds protection to the softer foams too.

Common names are extruded polystyrene or extruded-foam insulation board. A denser harder foam is available from craft suppliers, often called blue foam (although confusingly, it is now often black) or craft foam.

EXPANDED POLYSTYRENE is generally found as packaging and is recognizable by the white bead structure. It is very soft, messy to work with as the beads are prone to static and stick everywhere, and it is not at all resistant to heat or solvents. It is, however, normally free in packaging, which is a major plus point. As I have a ready supply, I use it to bulk out scenery which will have other layers on top.

PIR FOAM is fire resistant so cannot be cut with hot wire tools, but it is easily cut with a kitchen knife, although builders often use reciprocating saws. I recommend peeling the aluminium cover layer off as it can cause electrical shorts that can be very tricky to track down. It is messier than using hot wire tools on XPS foam as it creates lots of dust when carved, and is more powdery in texture.

I find the surface is quite crumbly, and it is easy to damage and rub off paint. I would therefore add a finish layer on top or seal well with PVA (white) glue. This foam can be glued with hot glue, Gorilla glue or white glue (if you allow extra time for it to dry as white glue needs air to set) as well as spray and specialist adhesives from the building trade. A common brand name is Celotex.

It is also easy to break (using a knife blade) into rock faces and we will look at that in Chapter 6.

HOT WIRE TRICKS This river bank was carved directly into the foam with a hot wire tool, then painted with artists' acrylic paints and a small amount of tile grout and earth blown onto it. I liked the effect of the hot wire, so you can still see the cutting marks from the tool in the finished scene.

FINISH COAT Foam will normally need a finish layer to add finer sculpting, support and protection. My preferred option is Sculptamold, which is a mix of plaster and paper pulp. It is lightweight but solid when dry. It is one of the easiest products to use and can be mixed to a range of consistencies. It can also be smoothed as it dries or left relatively lumpy if a texture is desired. You can add paint while mixing it so that it dries colored, which is an advantage if the area is likely to get heavy use and could be chipped.

It can be quite pricey in some countries, but there are homemade options on the internet.

STACKED AND CARVED Foam is one of the easiest products to work with. This section of scenery used XPS foam stacked in layers and carved with hot wire tools into a rough shape. The straight flat sections will be a river bed and weir.

HARD SHELL BASE LAYERS

● These tend to have two components, a base layer such as a cardboard web or crumpled paper, then the hard shell layer itself. I favor plaster cloth for this as it is easy to use and relatively mess free.

WOVEN WEB For large areas of scenery, perhaps with access needed behind a hillside, then a cardboard web is an easy base layer. Cardboard boxes can be cut up, curved in your hands and then hot glued or stapled in place. I start with contour boards every few feet—often made from cardboard or foam core—so that I have the outline I need. Then I hot glue the vertical strips in place. Finally, I weave horizontal strips back and fore and hot glue them in place.

This is a cheap, quick and reliable method for filling large spaces before you add a top layer.

SCRUNCHED PAPER If I am using plaster cloth, then I do not need much support beneath it, but I do need something so the cloth does not just lie flat. I may use lumps of foam, but crumpled paper is quick and easy. This is packing paper from an online purchase that is scrunched up. If you are worried about humidity or rodents, then bubble wrap or foil are other options. The purpose is merely to provide a base to drape the next hard shell layer over.

The paper can be removed once the next layer is in, but for vertical surfaces, I generally use hot glue to keep it in place as it is easier during the next stage.

STEP BY STEP • PLASTER CLOTH

Both of these mountainsides were built using plaster cloth over crumpled paper and foam scraps. I laid them on their backs during construction as they were not on a layout. Very little of the mountainside is seen, but this lightweight build works well as a base for scenery.

A VIEW INSIDE I cut away this portion of hillside to accommodate a change to my track layout. You can clearly see the construction with crumpled paper and layers of plaster cloth. Since I was pushing in trees in this area, I chose to do three or four layers of plaster cloth so there was a firmer base for the vegetation. I added a thin slurry of green colored plaster on top of the plaster cloth to fill in the holes, and threw on some ground foam as it will be a while before this particular section will be finished further. Plaster cloth is easy to make changes to compared to the more solid Sculptamold.

1 Plaster cloth is my favorite hard shell scenery material because it is relatively cheap and takes little time to cover large areas. I used scraps of foam and stiff crumpled paper to form the base layer. At this stage it is very rough and not at all robust. You can hot glue vertical pieces in place if you are working on your layout.

2 I like to lay the plaster cloth dry, then spray with water, which is much less messy than dipping it in water and dripping everywhere. I take advantage of the fact that the first layer can remain relatively stiff if you spray less water on it, so I laid long pieces across from contour board to contour board. If I am working on the layout, I work vertically by securing the top and letting the cloth hang downward before spraying with water.

3 I always do two layers. It is best to wait until the first layer has set but is not yet dry. I use smaller 6-inch squares of plaster cloth to add a much stronger overlapping second layer. I wet these a lot more than the first layer so that they bond to each other and the layer underneath. If your first layer is dry, then you should spray it with water again before laying the second layer to ensure a good bond between layers.

Plaster cloth does have small holes even when smoothed so the next step is to cover these. I use a thick earth layer, which also adds a lot more strength. We will cover that in detail in Chapter 7. However, a thin skim of Sculptamold will also work well. When using it over plaster products, I mix it more thinly as the plaster draws water out of it very quickly.

This diorama is built on one single layer of shaper sheet. The beach and vegetation were added directly on top of the shaper sheet plaster and it has provided a firm base.

OTHER HARD SHELL OPTIONS

There are far more options available than just plaster cloth, and modelers have been experimenting and trying new methods since the start of modeling.

Some of the classic options are:
- Plaster soaked paper towels or handiwipes or j-cloths (single ply so layers bond)—messier but very cheap if cost is an issue
- Paper mache with white glue—also a cheap option. I often use cheap card with white glue to add protection in flat areas of foam scenery
- Cloth with latex caulk as shown by Greg Condon in the photo at right

If you are using a material that is white, you can pre-color with paint, which will mean chips are less noticeable. It is worth experimenting to ensure that it still sets as you expect.

CHAPTER FOUR

Track

Track is the reason we model, so a key part of our scenery work is to make sure that our track is a realistic model too. Whether our track is handlaid or commercial, there are a number of improvements we can make to add realism, such as painting and ballast. Some of these details need to be factored in when we are laying the track. Those include allowing for drainage ditches, and the correct roadbed profile with perhaps a lower profile for sidings compared to the main line.

Track is scenery that works

Track, like all scenery, does not need to have as much detail where it is less visible. Distant tracks may just receive a simple paint job, where tracks right at the foreground could have more details such as rail joint bars and more comprehensive paint, picking out finer details with highlights or rust spots.

Before you start thinking of your track as scenery, though, it needs to be running flawlessly. Once it is ballasted in place, it becomes much harder to make adjustments. I tend to paint my track and ensure it is running again before adding all my ground layers. I ballast my track at this point as it allows the ballast to sit on top of the surrounding ground correctly. I like to add static grass in an area later because the grass is springy and it is hard to ballast over the top properly. It is also easier to ballast track before surrounding vegetation and buildings go in and block easy access.

You will need to protect your track if you are spraying scenic glue in an area. I use masking tape or just pieces of paper as blocks to prevent overspray gumming up any key workings.

LETTING TRACK TELL ITS STORY Track is vital to a model railroad and is a key part of the scenery. Pelle Søeborg has used ballast to delineate his main line from his siding. Weeds, junk, litter and a mixture of ground textures all add to the scene but the rails and ballast themselves are painted and weathered realistically.
Pelle Søeborg

BALLAST

Ballast choice is a key part of ensuring a realistic looking railroad scene. I like to use fine ballast on my HO layout because the stone size seems right to me in photos. Standard U.S. sizes are between 1 inch and 3$^{1}/_{2}$ inches, which scales to fine ballast in the Woodland Scenics range, although other brands have different sizing. For variety, you can lay your main line in a larger ballast and your sidings in a finer ballast or cinders. The key is to try a section and see if it looks like the photos of the area and time that you are modeling. In larger scales, chinchilla dust or aquarium gravel can also be used.

Many tracks away from the main line have very poor or cheap ballast. If you are modeling a yard, consider using cinders, ash or sand, and even black or gray colored tile grout. For urban areas, track set into roads or docks are prevalent (see Chapter 8 for examples). For my Welsh slate layout, fine slate chippings from the garden center will be used. These have been sieved into various grades, and even the smallest bag will last me a lifetime.

Ballast made from stone has weight so can be easier to lay as it sits into the ties better. I use Woodland Scenics and have not had an issue, but it is much lighter as it is made from crushed walnut shells. This means it bounces around during laying and is more easily displaced during gluing. However, its lightweight properties are an advantage for anyone modeling portable layouts.

BALLAST PROFILES Richard Bougerie and Warner Clark capture the typical ballast profile of a main line with a raised section beneath the rails, drainage to the sides and here, cinders at the very edges. Their Maumee Basin layout is Proto:48 with fine scale O scale track. *Richard Bougerie*

BALLAST MATERIALS Not all ballast is stone. If a suitable material is available, then it will be used. For example, yards frequently have cinders, and quarries use the available waste. My steam servicing yard is made of black and gray tile grout, Woodland Scenics fine and medium cinders, plus real wood ash around the ash pits.

MIXED MATERIALS Mike Confalone used a mix of dirt, sand and earth-toned tile grout to create a gravel mixture for a quarry on his Hardwick & Woodbury Division. He also used this mix to realistically ballast the track running into the quarry. *Mike Confalone*

• Basic ballasting

This is a step by step on ballasting so it will start with the assumption that your track is laid and running well. Once the ballast is in and glued, it is harder to fix mistakes or running issues. You will also want to add any trackwork details before starting these steps.

Track is a feature and where there is a small amount on a diorama, adding fishplates or any missing tie plates, spikes, ties, etc. will make a difference. Most of us are ballasting significant lengths of track, though, so we will be looking for the simplest option.

I have chosen not to raise the roadbed in this step by step, which is consistent with photographs of the branch line in this area. If you are modeling a siding next to a main line, then different track and ballast heights can help differentiate the two.

Additionally, the buildings in this area abut the track and are not finished yet, so I have not added the tile grout earth layer. As this ballast is embedded in the ground, this will not be an issue, but if you are doing a main line where the ballast spills over the surrounding ground, you will want to have finished at least the ground layer before ballasting. Ballasting over static grass is hard as it is quite springy, so I recommend doing static grass after ballasting.

Ballast choice is key to realism. There are many commercial options available, some from real stone and some from other products. You can also use materials such as chinchilla dust or talus. I prefer the same scenery glues as I use on all my scenery, but you can buy dry glues to mix with the ballast making the gluing stage easier and faster. For long sections of track, a ballast applicator can speed up the process with a little practice.

STEP BY STEP • PAINTING AND BALLASTING

1 Laying track often leaves holes from feeder wires, so I make sure that the ballast will not fall down these holes. You can use a filler, but I often just put a small piece of masking tape over the top. You can also protect key areas of turnouts at the same time with masking tape. I always wire my switch points so I am not relying on metal-to-metal contact for the electrical current to pass, but if you are relying on this, then do take care to mask out any required areas.

2 Before starting to paint, fill in any missing ties and any track details that you want to add. Joint bars or fish plates are available from several manufacturers. To replace missing ties, you can thin pieces leftover from laying flextrack, or buy ties just for the purpose.

3 Paint all the track including the rails with a brown color if ties are wooden, or a concrete color if that is appropriate. Depending on the age of the ties, wood may be more gray or a darker brown. Following a photo of track in the area you are modeling is the safest way to get the colors right. I chose Tamiya XF-72 Brown/JGSDF as the paint is quite tough—important when working with ballast—and the color matches the lightest color of the ties in this area.

4 The track here has a very rusty look, so I chose AK Interactive Rust Streaks AK7002 to represent that. An enamel wash such as this will flow easily into all the details and color both the rails and the tie plates and spikes. A heavily used area will have a darker color to the rail and metal anchors, and this stage can be adapted to suit. If the rails in your area is more or less the same color as the ties, then you could skip this stage and go straight to the dark wash.
This does not have to be neat as the next step will soften the edges of the rust wash.

4 To bring out the detail of the track and to help merge the rust wash, I add a dark enamel wash over the whole of the ties. This is thinner than the rust streaks and will flow into any cracks. It will also darken the ties to the color I was hoping for.

5 Once the paint and washes are dry, there are a number of ways of applying ballast, and one of the newer innovative ways is this applicator I found on eBay. If you have a lot of track to lay then it could be a real timesaver, although my attempt here put far too much down in one go!

6 I tend to stick to the old-fashioned teaspoon method and try to put a little less ballast on than I think I will need, which makes it easier to get off the ties.

7 I use a paint brush to spread the ballast. Ballast on ties is frequently pointed out as a flaw on model railroads, but look at the photos of your area in your timeframe as modern day UK sleepers are often covered in ballast.

STEP BY STEP • PAINTING AND BALLASTING

8 It can be quite a tedious process removing every last stray piece of ballast from around the spikes and the tops of ties. I use a brush to remove most of it, but as this is a very light ballast, it does not get the clean look I am after.

9 I use my finger dragged over the top of the ties to get the last pieces off and you can also tap the top of the rails to help settle the ballast down.

10 Once you have the ballast in the perfect position, it is important not to move it around when gluing. I use the same glues as for my scenery. I start with a fine spray of dilute isopropyl alcohol to help the ballast settle and break the surface tension before adding a spray of dilute matte Mod Podge. Wetting the ballast with a fine spray reduces the chances of making it move around in the next step.

11 A spray alone will often not reach the bottom layers of the ballast, leading to problems later on. I like to drip on more dilute matte Mod Podge starting along the edges as the glue will wick into the ballast and will not disturb it. I then drip along the rails as these break the fall of the drops and help it to spread evenly before I finally drop glue along the center of the ties. I found the dropper bottle on Amazon. By this point the ballast is already fairly damp so is less likely to be disturbed. When ballasting turnouts, I recommend regularly moving the switch points to avoid them getting stuck. If they do gum up, soaking the area with water will normally help loosen the glue.

12 Once the glue is dry, I rub my finger over the ties to remove any stray pieces of ballast and use a toothpick to remove them from around the spikes. Do take care with this as you can easily scrape the paint off.

13 Track is often weathered, especially in areas where locomotives sit for long periods. The photos of this track showed a lighter streak down the middle, so I used a light dust pigment to represent this.

14 Normally I would use a darker pigment, such as this dark earth, or a dark tile grout. You can also use charcoal. For these darker colors, I try to wipe a lot off my brush before applying to the ballast as it grabs the pigments, easily leading to unwanted dark patches. It is better to build it up gradually as it is hard to remove excess dark colors.

15 I find a damp finger helps tone down the pastel application to give a more realistic look.

STEP BY STEP • PAINTING AND BALLASTING

16 Finally, I clean the rail heads. Here I have used a paper towel wrapped around a sanding block and soaked in isopropyl alcohol, which removes all the paint very easily. A final pass with a dry piece of paper towel and it is ready to go.

17 This is the final stretch of plain track. If you do have any issues, then soaking with water will normally loosen the ballast making it easier to remove. When I finally add the surrounding earth layers, I will blend them in with the ballast. The grass runs right up to the edge of the ballast, which will further hide the transition.

● Details

Once your track and ballast are laid you can start adding the final details. These include ash, sand and oil stains in servicing areas, cigarette butts and tea bags (in the UK) around workmen's huts, weeds, litter, cans, and bottles. Lance Mindheim even added a dead chicken to his!

TRACK BECOMES A FOCAL POINT Lance Mindheim's Miami's Downtown Spur features sidings inset into concrete with weeds and stones, adding a lot of character to a simple piece of track. Chapter 8 includes information about setting track in streets.
Lance Mindheim

CHAPTER FIVE

Backdrops

Layouts are almost always constrained by space, and a backdrop helps create the world beyond the layout we cannot fit in the available space. Sometimes this is as simple as a blue painted sky, sometimes it is a complete 3D model with forced perspective and integral LED lighting so it is impossible to work out where the layout ends and the backdrop starts.

EXPAND YOUR VIEW Backdrops bring the world beyond to a layout and ensure that the viewer is not distracted by unwanted clutter that destroys the illusion of being there—but you do not need to be an artist to achieve that. *Paul J. Dolkos*

Containing the scene

Backdrops also play a vital role in hiding the extraneous clutter that exists in most layout rooms. The eye will largely ignore a plain white wall behind a layout, but windows, doors, and cupboards can be huge distractions, even more so in photographs. The aim of a layout is to re-create a slice of real life in miniature, and the backdrop will help reinforce that.

One key point is that the backdrop is not the main star of your layout. When choosing colors, photographs and details, care must be given to ensuring they do not grab the eye more than the layout itself. Not everyone adds backdrops, though, and peninsulas will often not have them. In this case, the rest of the layout may act as a backdrop.

SETTING THE SCENE

A simple piece of blue painted foam core shows the difference that even a simple backdrop makes to a layout.

TYPES OF BACKDROPS

SIMPLE SOLUTION The simplest backdrop is a painted sky. A paler color, such as on Lance Mindheim's CSX Miami Downtown Spur, does not grab attention away from the layout. It is also easy to replace in photo editing software if you want to add a more dramatic sky from a real photo. *Lance Mindheim*

BLENDING DISTRACTIONS Rolf Plachter has painted the ductwork that so often accompanies ceilings in a basement the same color as his sky, helping it disappear at first glance. The black fascia and curtains help finish the bottom of the layout. *Cody Grivno*

LAYOUT AS BACKDROP Dick Elwell's Hoosac Valley layout sweeps back and fore across a 64-foot deep basement. Many of his peninsulas do not have backdrops, but Dick has made great use of the farthest part of his basement to act as a backdrop for the nearer sections giving a depth that could not otherwise be achieved. *Bob Van Gelder*

PHOTO BACKDROPS Photographic backdrops have become more and more prevalent and they can either be bought commercially or printed from your own photos, as here on Pelle Søeborg's layout. Note the valence above and fascia below, which will help frame the scene. *Pelle Søeborg*

COMBINED ELEMENTS Bob Lawson's Rathole Division of the Southern Railway combines sky, mountains and 3D elements to add great depth in a few inches and create realistic scenes. *Lou Sassi*

PRACTICAL ISSUES

● Materials

The first step in planning is to decide on the construction method and materials. Backdrops can be a series of layers, such as sky images overlaid with mountains and more detailed photos. The very basic first layer is normally sky and needs to be as seamless as possible to avoid vertical lines across the sky. I recommend coving corners where possible so there are no straight lines or dark corners with obvious differences in sky color between two walls caused by variations in the angle the light is striking them.

The most basic backdrop is to use the plaster walls of a room and to add coving into the corner using one of the materials discussed below. Where a whole backdrop is needed there are a number of options.

The most common product will be wood based and I favor those with minimal surface texture as they give better results. Medium density fiberboard (MDF) or hardboard (Masonite) are examples that work well. Flexible MDF can be used in corners. To prevent gaps at the seams between sheets, drywall tape and joint compound can be used; I have also used flexible filler which has some allowance for expansion.

Sheet signage plastic, such as foamex, a foamed PVC board, is a great product as it is easy to cut, comes in large flexible sheets, and paints well to a nice smooth finish.

Smaller layouts can use a wider range of materials from sheet PIR or XPS foam, sheet aluminium, foam core, or even card. Lining wallpaper can be used on top of textured backdrop materials, such as plywood, to give a smooth matt surface which takes paint well.

Warping can be an issue with lightweight materials that are wood- or paper-based, and I find treating the front and back identically helps eliminate this. That means that if you paint the front of foam core, it will warp, but if you paint the back as well, it will remain straighter. Finally, small layouts and dioramas can even be taken outside and a real view used as the ultimate realistic backdrop.

SHARP CORNERS
When I initially decided to add an alcove into the backdrop for a cameo scene, I used straight corners with no coving. In every photo, the straight lines were very visible and distracting.

SOFT EDGES
I updated this corner with not only flowing curved corners but also with additional LED lighting to ensure that the corner was not darker than the surrounding backdrop. A smokestack was used to hide the very sharp front right corner, just visible above the car float structure. Also visible in the back right of this photo is an acetate panel that is very handy for keeping elbows from demolishing delicate parts of scenery.

SMOOTH SURFACE
Hardboard (Masonite) is one of the most common materials as it is flexible, easy to use, and readily available. Jim Reising used tempered hardboard attached to the walls with screws on his Oakville Sub layout. He coved the corners and added printed backdrops from Backdrop Warehouse.
Jim Reising

DISSIMILAR MATERIALS My first layout used signage plastic for its backdrop. It was easy to cut and install and the only snag for me was its expansion and contraction in my layout room, which has large temperature fluctuations through the year. It looked great initially but it developed noticeable gaps in the colder winter months as can be seen in the photo above. For smaller layouts needing only one piece or in more temperature controlled rooms, this is an ideal product.

NATURAL BACKDROPS Sunlight can give very realistic photographic results. It was very easy to take this 1-foot square diorama into my backyard to use real light and vegetation as a backdrop. Exhibition or portable layouts can also be taken outside, although this is impractical for fixed layouts.

METAL Lance Mindheim used aluminium trim coil to create a long seamless backdrop for this layout. *Lance Mindheim*

PRACTICAL ISSUES

● Lighting

Good lighting will show off your layout to its best and while this is a book on scenery, it is important to ensure your lighting is even. When planning your lighting, bear in mind that spotlights can leave brighter and darker spots on a backdrop. The position of lighting is key to avoid leaving the front of the layout in darkness but also to avoid casting shadows of buildings and trees onto the backdrop, which destroy the illusion of the scene. This can be hard to avoid with typical overhead lighting, as in my layout, but I have added in strip LED lights in specific locations to ensure that dark corners or shadows are eliminated.

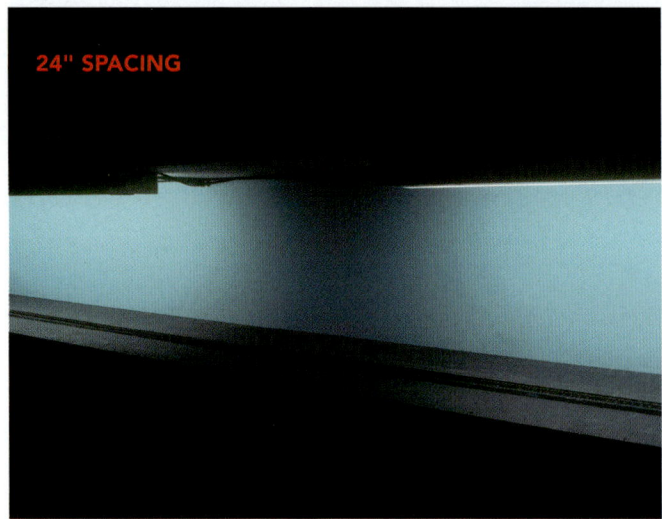
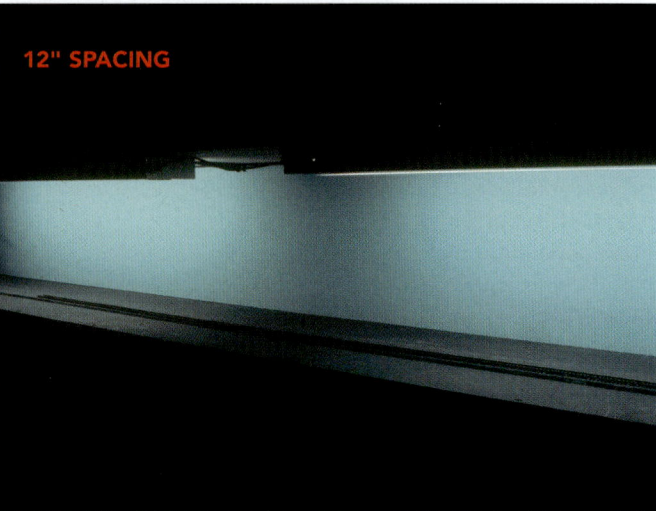
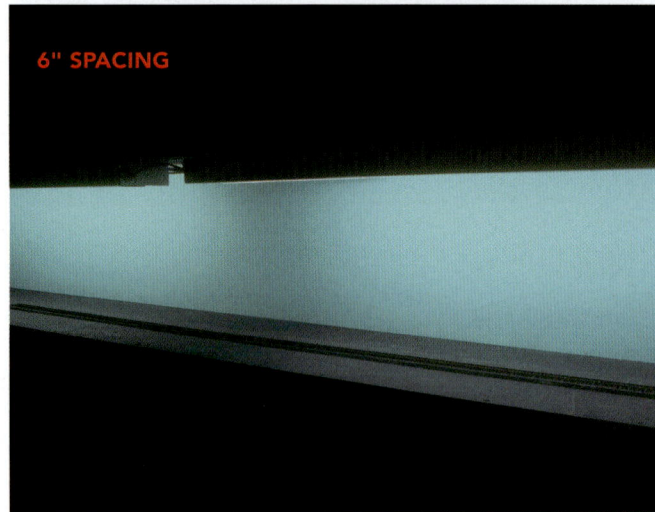
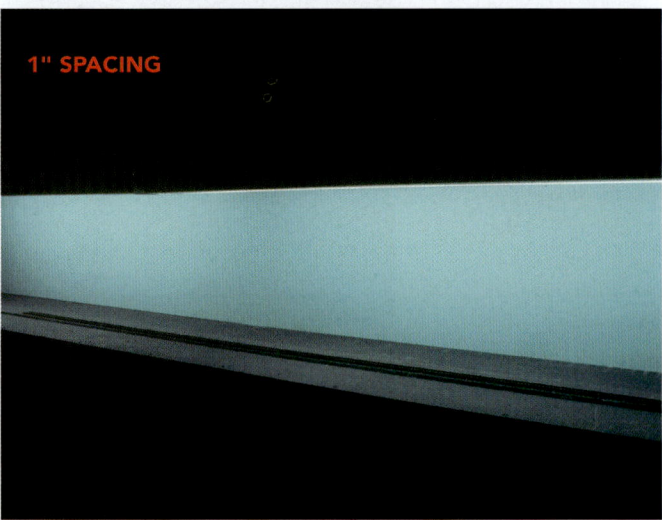

Tony Koester carried out an experiment by placing lighting fixtures at a number of distances apart. Even a small 6-inch gap between fixtures gave a noticeable shadow effect on the backdrop. *Tony Koester*

● Height

Once the materials are decided, the next consideration is the backdrop height. These are often set by the room itself, but I have found that tall backdrops give a wider range of shots when taking photos. However, an upper level or awkward room shape may limit the options.

Where there are no limits to height, use a camera to check there will be no awkward gaps at the top of key scenes. Also consider the heights of your viewers and friends. For a tall layout, shorter people, such as children, will see more of the backdrop as they look up at it, whereas taller people will tend to look across. It is worth ducking down if you are tall to consider other viewpoints.

FASCIAS, VALENCES AND STAGE EXITS

In many ways, our layouts are like miniature theaters with our trains as the actors and our layouts as the theater scenery. One trick we can steal from theaters is the use of fascias and valences to frame the view of the audience, see page 49. I prefer a theater-type black fascia below the layout and valence above. The valence acts as a natural end to the sky and blocks any lighting from shining into the eyes of the viewers. The height of the valence above the layout should bear in mind those shorter viewers, but not crop out the view completely for taller visitors. All this will be dependent on the height of the layout itself above the ground. The viewing gap on my upper deck is much smaller than the lower deck because of the angles of standing and sitting visitors.

The final practical consideration is how trains enter and exit through a backdrop. Many layouts will have hidden staging yards and the trains need to move into the scenic area without giving away the illusion. The easiest way is for the train to emerge from a tunnel or from behind a building or wooded area so that it naturally appears. However, if this is not possible, continuing the scenery into the start of the staging area can tie the two areas together.

CONTINUING SCENES Bob Smaus added building flats on his Southern Pacific layout (top) into the start of his staging yard so the city appeared to continue far beyond the scenic part of the layout. *Bob Smaus*

BOARD GAMES James McNab demonstrated on Model Railroader Video Plus (now Trains.com) that space does not have to be an issue (middle). His staging area is hidden by a removable board. The photographic backdrop continues onto the board, which can easily be put in place to hide his staging area. *James McNab*

LIGHTS Paul Dolkos added lights to his staging area beyond the highway bridge to avoid it appearing as a black hole (bottom). *Paul J. Dolkos*

SKY THEORY

● **Lighting**

The starting point of most backdrops is the sky, and at its simplest, you can just add blue paint. One key concept is that the backdrop should not distract from the layout itself. If possible, colors should be slightly more muted and the modeling less detailed so the eye refocuses itself back to the main part of the layout. This is especially true of the choice of sky color. I used a fairly bright color when I first painted my layout sky, and it was just too bright. After years of living with it, I chose a more muted color from a photo and repainted the sky. Now the sky recedes rather than grabbing your attention and the whole layout seems more realistic.

FADE AND PERSPECTIVE Painting successful skies needs two key elements: the blue fades as it gets closer to the horizon and clouds get smaller as they get farther away, that is lower down in the sky.

DIMINISHING DETAIL Not only does the sky color fade toward the horizon in this photo of Tehachapi, but the background hills also fade in color intensity and toward a bluer color in the farther distance. The foreground is also very sharp, but mountains are much less detailed and not in focus. We can emulate this effect with our backdrops. Chapter 1 considered the need for a layout color palette and the backdrop colors need to match the layout color tones, especially if vegetation is being represented on both.

PAINTED BACKDROPS

● Painting a backdrop is the simplest method for adding sky. As the sky can take up quite a large surface area, emulsion or latex house paints are the easiest option in most cases. A suitable shade can be color matched to a photo in most DIY stores if none of the commercial ranges have the right shade. I find using a small paint roller the easiest way to paint a smooth sky color.

If your scenery is very high, such as in a large city or mountain valley, you may be able to paint it more or less the same color blue, but in most instances you will need to fade the blue to the horizon. This can be quite tricky to blend well at first, but with practice, it does get easier. I tend to use a brush and mix the paint colors on the backdrop by hand. If you have access to a large sprayer, then it is easier to achieve a much more sophisticated gradient.

BRUSH Hand-painting a gradient from sky blue to a paler shade at the horizon will take practice. The trick is to ensure the paints remain wet so they can be blended. Pelle Søeborg used oil paints to ensure he had plenty of time to work on the paint and mixed six colors to get a constant even transition. *Pelle Søeborg*

SPRAY Gerry Leone used an airless sprayer to first paint a sky blue paint layer, then add an atmospheric haze at the bottom using a paler blue. *Gerry Leone*

DIGITAL TRICKS An easy way to check a color is to use an eye dropper tool in a photo editing program to isolate one area of color. This is useful when picking a color to get a custom mixed paint color from a DIY store.

ANALOG You can pick the same color from the photo by using a sheet of paper with a small hole cut out of it to isolate the color without any distractions. You can paint colors next to it until you match it exactly. Be sure to check the paint colors with the layout lighting as it may make the colors appear different.

NOT ALWAYS BLUE Not every day is sunny and I have enjoyed painting gray skies as much as blue. My first U.S. layout had very stormy skies, but they were easy to paint and set a very different tone to most layouts.

DETAILED PAINTING Painting backdrops goes beyond just skies and, depending on your skills, can range from a distant background mountain to a full blown work of art. Lee Marsh painted these mountains on Masonite using photos for reference. He added some snow and mounted the backdrop an inch away from the sky to give the illusion of added distance. *Lee Marsh*

CLOUD PRACTICE Clouds can add interest to a backdrop, and in some parts of the world are the usual view. They may appear daunting, but with a little practice are easy to add. Matt Carpenter's son, Sam, painted this backdrop on his N scale Rio Grande layout. *Cody Grivno*

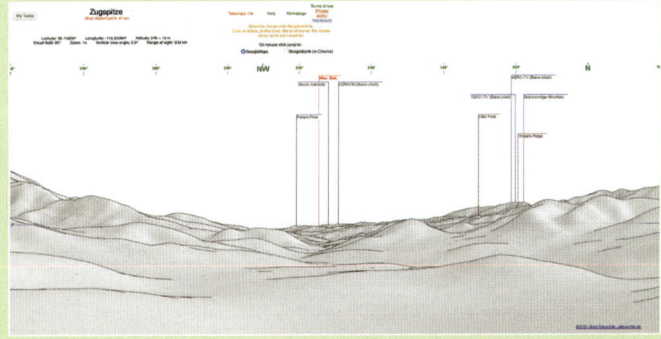

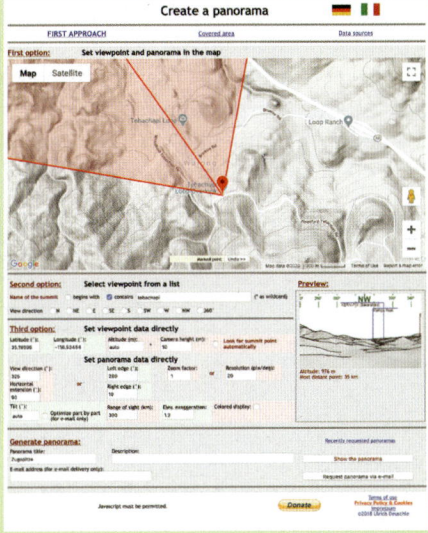

DIGITAL REFERENCE Modeling distant locations with no available photos is not an issue today. Google Earth provides great reference photos from roads, but one handy website to help with shaping backdrop scenery is https://www.udeuschle.de/panoramas/makepanoramas_en.htm. It gives a panoramic view of the scenery at a given location, and does not have to be on a road. I have used the same location as the photo of Tehachapi Loop earlier in the chapter, but it is also very useful for coastal locations and a view inland from the sea.

57

STEP BY STEP • SKIES & CLOUDS

PAINT BRUSH CLOUDS

I needed a few backdrops for my portable layouts and dioramas so I painted one in a blue gradient, one with brush-painted clouds, and one with airbrushed clouds using a stencil.

1 I used emulsion (latex) paints, as backdrops are generally large areas. This was a color matched blue paint from my local DIY store. I also used white. I first painted 2/3 of the board in blue.

2 Using the same brush I painted the blue with, I dipped it in the white paint and painted the lower strip of the board. The blue paint already on the brush colors the white so it becomes a pale blue. I work up the bottom 1/3 of the board, mixing white and blue as I go. The colors need to get darker as the paint gets farther up with the final coat being pure blue to match the top of the board. This can be tricky to judge as the blue dries darker than when it is wet, but practice will help.

3 The first coat is often a little uneven and a second coat of all the colors will help even out the gradient. If the paints are not mixing well, then they can be thinned slightly. It is important that the paints remain wet while the gradient is being painted.

4 I sketch in the clouds using a photo as reference. I am using the white emulsion (latex) paint and a ½-inch chip brush.

5 I paint all the lightest areas in pure white emulsion paint.

6 Next I paint the darkest colors, adding artists' acrylic colors to tint the emulsion paint. I find neutral gray and Payne's gray to be the best colors, but it is best not to go too dark.

7 Finally, I paint in the mid-tones using either grays or the sky blue to darken the white emulsion paint. I use the grays in the nearer larger clouds and the blue to fade the clouds as they become smaller and nearer the horizon line.

AIRBRUSH CLOUDS

1 Airbrushes are perfect for painting clouds as they can give a lovely wispy effect. If you are not sure about your airbrushing skills, then combine them with stencils to give the outline of the top of the cloud and paint beneath. I did this backdrop using spray paint.

I first painted a plain blue backdrop, then I added some spray at the bottom to represent the very distant clouds.

2 I designed this cloud shape, then cut this stencil from copy paper using an electronic craft cutter. There is a bit of overspray from a spray can which can ruin the effect, so adding extra sheets of paper to block the blue areas is important.

3 Any white spray paint will do, but you need to use light gentle strokes of paint. Spray from the direction of the stencil to avoid the paint blowing under the edge. A small gap is not an issue as it will avoid a really harsh top to the cloud.

4 Repeat until you have filled the area.

PHOTO BACKDROPS

● Photographic backdrops are an exciting way to add realistic background scenes. They can be mixed with a painted sky to add more depth to a layout, or can be used to create an entire backdrop including the sky. One of the biggest challenges to adding a photographic backdrop is finding suitable photos, especially if modeling historic periods. There are plenty of commercial backdrop companies with libraries of photos and backdrops. A number of websites, such as Google Maps, can provide suitable images. If you are modeling a historic era, then you can use black & white photos and color them. This works best on light colored buildings, but is an option when the modern era looks very different.

You can also use your own photographs to create custom backdrops. One further source of photos is the backs of your model buildings. These will match your layout modeling better than photos.

COMMERCIAL BACKDROPS These curved flowing backdrops on Bill Brown's layout show how effective photo backdrops can be. Bill's company, LARC products, provide large format landscape backdrops. *Lou Sassi*

ONLINE OPTIONS Google Earth (www.google.com/earth) gives detailed 3D views that are invaluable for planning layouts and particularly for obtaining photographic backdrops. The only issue can be the quality, which can be low resolution. *Google Earth*

DIY BACKDROPS I created this backdrop in Photoshop from a number of photos I had taken on a trip to New England. The photos are from many locations, but were added together to create a convincing backdrop. The sky color matches my layout, so any blue in the tree foliage matched when I cut it out. I ensured that the background photos were not too sharp so they looked at a focus level consistent with a distant scene. I also lightened and changed the saturation so the photos all looked consistent. I then printed this onto a number of sheets of A3 copy paper and glued it with glue sticks to my sky-painted backdrop. A professional print shop will give a more robust print with better depth of color. Printing on a matte finish paper is recommended.

PHOTO TIPS Consider taking your own photos for a backdrop if you can get access to a similar spot or, better still, the real location. Take photos in portrait mode where possible with 30 percent overlap and on the same camera settings (use manual settings and do not use a polarizing filter). Software like Photoshop will stitch them together seamlessly. You can then crop or clone out any unwanted features or foreground.

COLORIZING IMAGES We are often modeling eras when photography was primarily black & white, and it can be challenging to find suitable photos. We can sometimes use modern images and remove any items later than the period we are modeling, but what if the areas are completely different? Today, we can use software to recolor black & white images so we can use them in photographic backdrops.

MyHeritage—https://www.myheritage.com/incolor is a website that will colorize black & white photos, and will also restore color in photos if you have a faded color photograph. You will need to register to use this site, but it is free. It gives the best results based on the sites I have tested, but there are plenty of options available.

3D BACKDROPS

- Backdrops can be many layers with the sky and photographic backdrops forming the back two layers. Adding multiple layers can achieve great depth of scenery in a relatively short space. Chapter 1 covered forced perspective and backdrops are a natural way to achieve this.

The easiest way to add more depth is to start to introduce textures to the backdrop. This could be by adding relief to flat buildings using decoupage techniques, or by adding ground foam to thin card or foam core hillsides. As the backdrop becomes more and more detailed, it becomes hard to distinguish where the backdrop ends and the layout starts.

TEXTURE Simple hillsides can be made from ground foam sprinkled onto foam core. They add a little bit of texture. It can help to choose a duller or bluer color of green.

PUFFBALLS The name "puffball" trees does not do them justice. These hit all the right notes for a backdrop, modeling just the outline of the tree itself. They can be made in a variety of ways, but the most common is to roll a ball out of polyfiber, then to cover with spray adhesive and ground foam. Brooks Stover has used these on his S scale Buffalo Creek and Gauley layout as on the right-hand side here. *Brooks Stover*

MINI TREES This work-in-progress photo shows the background trees on my layout. These small trees are twisted wire Z and N scale trees bought in bulk. They are not the best looking when they arrive with lurid colors. I added ground foam to create a unified look across the hillside and mounted them by poking the wire trunks into a sheet of foam core. They flow down into larger mid-ground trees on a plaster cloth base. All the foam core and plaster cloth is covered in greenery to mask any gaps.

Other ideas for distant small evergreen trees include bumpy chenille pipe cleaners, or even cocktail sticks with ground foam glued on.

STACKING AND PACKING Low relief houses, buildings or vehicles can be used to add more buildings into a smaller space. Rick Van Laar demonstrates how the use of progressively shallower buildings towards the rear of his Rosston, Joelberg & Holly RR enables him to fit a whole town into a relatively small space. *Lou Sassi*

STRUCTURES Perspective is more of an issue with backdrop buildings than with hills or vegetation. Ending a street in a T-junction is one solution as here on Paul Dolkos's Baltimore Harbor District layout. The trees also disrupt the perspective view making the two roads blend seamlessly. *Paul J. Dolkos*

VIEW BLOCKS The photographic backdrop and snow scenery on the other side of this bridge does not need to extend very far to either side as the viewer is blocked from seeing farther by the other side of the bridge. This can be useful when adding scenery to small areas such as alleys, streets, or under bridges.

3D BACKDROPS

BLENDING BACKDROPS Continuing foreground features onto the backdrop, such as hills, buildings and rivers, can ensure the layout appears to continue for miles. Tom Johnson carefully blended a photograph scene with his foreground road and trees. A slight bump in the pavement helps mask the joint between the horizontal road and the vertical photograph while the buildings prevent viewing from unrealistic angles. *Tom Johnson*

REFLECTIVE BACKDROPS Mirrors are an easy way to cheat some space on the layout by reflecting back the existing buildings or scenery. Careful attention to viewing angles is needed to ensure visitors cannot see themselves, and the edges must be hidden to maintain the illusion. Gerry Leone used 12 mirrors to great effect on one of his Bona Vista layouts. He hid the edges with natural changes in levels, buildings or vegetation. His key points for successful mirror usage are front-surface mirrors and ensuring 90 degree angles so that the reflections appear natural.

The left-hand photo shows a typical street scene extended with a mirror with the edges masked by buildings and a banner. The mirror reflects a photo of a street scene hidden within the building to the left.

The right-hand photo shows a mirror in a more rural setting. The front of the mirror is hidden by rapids in the water and the surrounding vegetation. *Gerry Leone*

FORCED PERSPECTIVE These two photos demonstrate a large 3D backdrop created by the Missenden Abbey team for the Great Model Railway Challenge. The photo backdrop includes LED lights and is taken from Google Maps. The perspective is carried on through the rows of terraced houses that are progressively smaller toward the rear. They are modeled in card so the printed size can be altered before printing to give a seamless feeling of forced perspective.

From the front, the perspective illusion gives great depth in the 5-foot-deep scene. From the side, the illusion is more visible. Forced perspective does rely on a fixed viewing point and city scenes are far more challenging than their rural equivalents because of the straight lines on every building.

BLENDING AND CONCEALING George Sellios is a master at making an entire city fit in a small space. He has even added smoke to his backdrop for extra realism using a mix of cotton and paint. George has used them to mask any seams in his backdrop, but they also add an industrial feeling to the scene. *Richard Josselyn*

CHAPTER SIX

Rocks and stones

Some scenery locations require majestic rock faces, such as this scene from the Greeley, Colo., museum, but even the most ordinary location requires some stones. *Robert Sobol*

Rocks and stones are everywhere, and they add vital height and texture to a scene. There are so many variations in strata, type, and erosion that it is vital to have good photos of the rocks in the area you are modeling so you can match both shape and color. I am not a geologist, so pictures are vitally important to me. The shapes will also determine the best way to model the scene.

An early addition

I find that adding rocks at the foundations stage is best so they are bedded into the scenery and especially the ground and earth layers. Large rocks and stones can be added at the same time. This is also the time to add large rock features to any water courses, such as rivers, if needed. River rocks are normally more rounded as they have been smoothed by the water running over them.

There are a multitude of methods to model rocks and new ones are being invented all the time. The methods generally fall into three sorts: molding, carving, and using bought or found materials. I tend toward lightweight materials because most of my layouts are moveable and weight is a real issue. This means foams, foam clay, or Sculptamold are key, but for small sections, all the methods are suitable.

For large areas, molding will produce a series of identical rock castings which, even when cut into pieces and rearranged, may start to be identifiable as a repeating pattern. Carving will generally produce more unique rocks as no one area is the same as anywhere else, but is perhaps the most daunting method. Natural items, such as cork or bark, will not have this issue as each piece is subtly different.

I once saw a layout made out of real rocks. It weighed a ton and the small rocks and pebbles were a different color than the rock faces, presumably because of what was available. Real rock, like water, is not necessarily better as it may not scale down well.

The same techniques discussed in this chapter for rock faces can also be used for a wide range of scenic elements such as retaining walls, bridge abutments, and river beds.

SHAPES OF ROCKS If we compare two rock outcrops from different locations, we can see how important it is to get the shapes right. This jagged and sliced stone is on the Fairfield Horseshoe in the Lake District, U.K., and is volcaniclastic sandstone. The colors are grays and there are lichens on the rock giving it a dappled appearance.

DESERT SCENE On the other side of the world in Joshua Tree National Park, Calif., the rock is gneiss and granite. The colors are warm and the rock shapes are rounded with smooth edges.

METHODS OF CASTING

COMMERCIAL MOLDS Casting is one of the easiest methods of creating great-looking rock faces. There is a huge variety of commercial molds to use in a range of different rock types. They can be used with a variety of materials such as plaster or resin and are my favorite method for realistic rockwork.

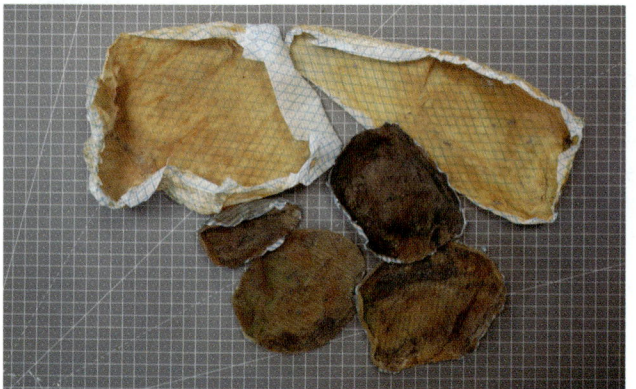

DIY MOLDS As well as purchasing molds, you can also make your own. There are two elements: the first is a suitable rock to cast. I have used coal as it has a nice, dense strata reminiscent of larger rocks. You can also 3D print a rock face to cast or use materials such as cork or bark. The second is the mold itself. This is normally built up with many thin layers of latex rubber with an outer jacket. I used J-cloths, a form of heavy disposable wipe, to add strength as the rubber is easy to tear. It is not a quick method as each layer has to fully air dry before the next layer can be added.

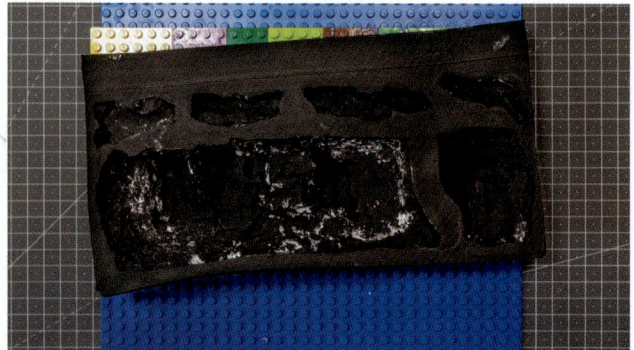

SUPPORT Some molds needs a bit of support to keep them level for casting and I use Lego bricks or weights for this.

CARVING

FOAM Carving requires a little more skill than casting, but is easily mastered. Foam is a great substance to carve as it is soft and can be carved with knives, hot tools, heat, or solvents. Plaster and Sculptamold can also be carved and it is easier to do so before the material is completely dry and cured.

SCULPTAMOLD can be carved to make realistic rocks, as shown by Leon Wasiak on this diorama. *Leon Wasiak*

PURCHASED ROCKS

There are some great commercial offerings available which can just be integrated into your layout. If you only want to cover small areas, or are after specific properties, then these can be a great option. Shown above are Noch hard foam rocks, rubber rocks, and Noch wrinkle rocks, which are printed paper on a foil backing that you just scrunch up and put in place.

CASTING MATERIALS

PLASTER CASTINGS are a stalwart of rock modeling. Not all plasters are created equal, and those such as Hydrocal or fine dental plaster will give better detailed casts. Plaster can be messy compared to some of the other materials, and some plasters are very heavy in large sections. To avoid white chips, you can pre-color the mix with a dark acrylic paint or ink.

SCULPTAMOLD is a key material when attaching plaster castings as it is used to fill the gaps between castings. It can be used as a casting material in its own right but I find it lacks detail.

EVA FOAM is a dense flexible foam that comes in sheets but is also commonly found as floor mats. It makes lightweight rocks, and is best carved with a Dremel-type motor tool. I use it for background rocks with a more eroded and rounded feel.

RESIN can be used to cast rocks in molds. It is lighter than plaster, although more expensive. It does produce very detailed castings and is much more robust. It will not easily chip, but can be colored before it is cast. You can use a foaming resin to fill out the back of the mold so that the more expensive casting resin is only used as a thin skin.

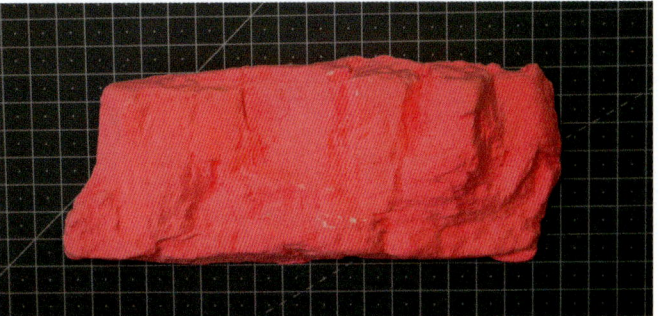

FOAM CLAY is a relatively new product and it is the lightest option. It can be used in molds if pressed in well. It will shrink slightly as it dries, but remains slightly flexible, which is useful when fitting. If demolding quickly is a priority, then the molds can be put in a freezer which firms up the foam clay enough to remove it straight away. It can then be left to air harden before use. It does come in white and black, but is also available more cheaply as a children's play item, hence this bright pink color.

MIXED MATERIALS

OPTIONS Techniques can easily be combined. Foam can be carved away to give large swaths of realistic rock, then coated with a product like Sculptamold to add rigidity. It is a great lightweight and relatively cheap method to cover large mountainsides. The *Model Railroader*/Model Railroader Video Plus team built the Canadian Canyons layout with three styles of rocks. They used carved extruded foam and Sculptamold, Mountains in Minutes foam rocks, and Cripplebush Valley rubber rocks to model all the various different types of rock. *William Zuback (three photos)*

MATERIALS

NATURAL ELEMENTS Bark, cork or charcoal pieces can all be used as rock faces. This scene by John Longhurst uses bark he found as a rock face. It was free, and no one piece is the same. Repetition can be a problem with using castings from the same mold many times on a layout.

Other modelers have successfully used compressed paper ceiling tiles for layered rock. There are many materials that can be used depending on the type of rock being modeled. *John Longhurst*

CARVED FOAM Foam is a very versatile material in all areas of modeling. Horst Meier carved these realistic rocks from foam and sealed them with a coating of white glue before painting as the foam remains soft unless protected.
Horst Meier

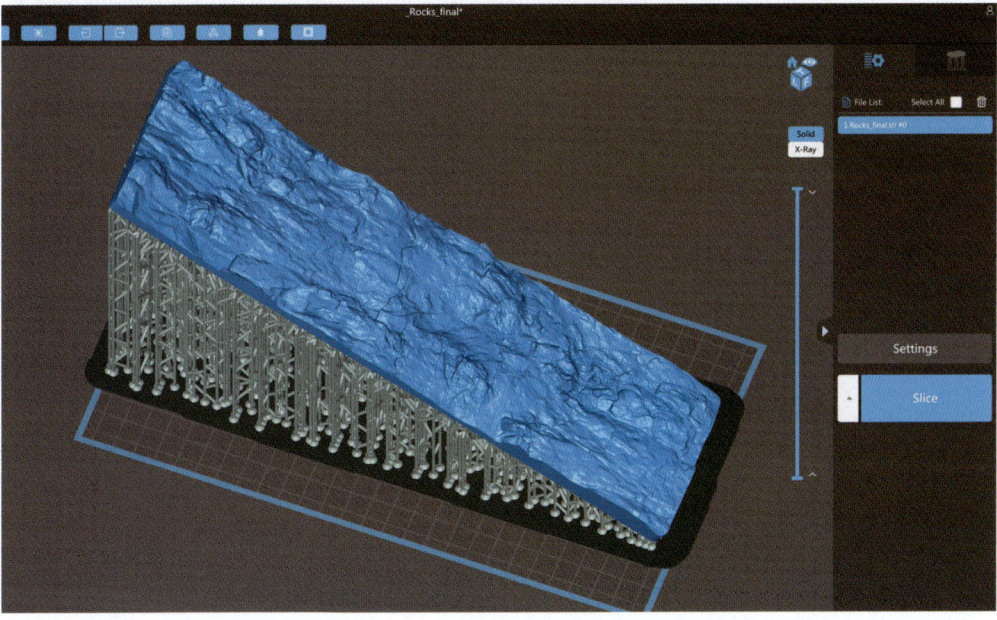

3D PRINTING is coming into every area of the hobby, and rock faces are another good example. I bought some rock brushes and used a free program, Blender, to make this rock face in a couple of minutes. This would not be a cheap option for a mountainside, but would be a great way to make your own castings using the 3D printed rocks, and opens up opportunities for rock types which do not have commercial molds available.

STEP BY STEP • CASTING

1 There are a wide variety of materials we have looked at for casting rocks, but this is the easiest, plaster. This is plain hobby shop plaster with a 2:1 mix, plaster to water. Do check the measurements as the ratios vary. I measure out all the ingredients and, as I have lost count in the past, I make sure I have the right number of cups of plaster for the water!

2 The plaster is poured into the water and left to settle before mixing. The water wicks up through the plaster and this leads to fewer lumps. Once all the plaster is absorbed, you can then mix thoroughly. I tend to do one cup at a time and there is enough working time to ensure that everything is thoroughly mixed.

3 I made a simple foil mold for this rock face. You can just crumple up aluminium foil, although it requires some practice to achieve a realistic rock face.

4 Spraying with water or adding talcum powder before the plaster is poured in will help release the surface tension and ensure that the plaster fills all the small details. Alternatively, a brush can be used to help it into any particularly difficult areas. Then it is left to set.

5 Plaster will set from a chemical reaction fairly quickly, although the different types and brands vary. Once set, you can demold and use the casting, although it will be a while longer before it is completely dry. You can place the casting into the scene before it is fully set so it can be bent to conform to the scenic contours. The correct point in time to do this will take a bit of practice but once the plaster does not run out of the mold, you can put it into place and hold it until it sets. This technique is best carried out with quick setting plasters, such as Hydrocal.

6 You can "glue" castings in place with Sculptamold, more plaster, or hot glue. My favorite is Sculptamold, and here I am using it between many castings that form a large outcrop.

STEP BY STEP • CARVING

1 Rocks carved from foam are easy to create, cheap, and very lightweight. They can cover large mountainsides with little effort. This is PIR foam and has a fairly crumbly texture. You can use a wide variety of tools to carve rocks, from kitchen carving knives, such as here, to specialist carving tools. The knife tip is being used to split out sections leaving a very realistic texture on the foam.

2 Eroded or layered rocks can be modeled in a matter of minutes. Once the rough shape is carved, a wire brush will add the rock strata. I first drew it down in short, sharp, strokes to add a little detail, then I dragged the brush horizontally in long strokes to add the layer lines. I finished off by brushing with a paint brush and using a vacuum cleaner to remove the powdery dust left behind.

3 This foam is very soft so needs to be sealed to prevent the paint from just rubbing off later. I use a diluted white glue mix, which is thin enough to not leave brush strokes or to mask the foam texture. I applied three thin coats before painting. I used the painting steps following with burnt sienna and raw umber base coats, a black wash, and a pale umber dry brush to finish the rock. The finished rock in shown under Carving on page 70.

STEP BY STEP • PAINTING

The rocks are plaster cast in Woodland Scenics molds and painted using the following step by step.

1 Before we start on the rock faces, we need to pick a base color. I generally do two base coats to get enough coverage. The first is often a generic shade straight out of the bottle. My two favorites are raw umber (here) and warm gray. I use artists acrylic paints thinned to a consistency that no longer shows the brush strokes when painted on. I use this color all over my rocks and ground layer (here Sculptamold) and both will soak up the first layer of paint, so a thinner mix is better. For the second paint layer, I custom mixed a brown that matched a photo of the rocks I was painting.

2 I drybrush a lighter mix of the brown all over the high points of the rocks. This brings out the detail in the castings.

3 I added a wash made from india ink diluted in isopropyl alcohol over the rock face which settles into all the cracks.

4 At this point, you can stop if you are happy with the coloring. I was not completely satisfied that my rocks matched the photos, so I added more drybrushing in a slightly lighter color. With gray rocks, I often drybrush slightly different shades of blues, greens and browns to add variety.

5 This is an acrylic black wash brushed over the surface to bring some more depth to the cracks.

6 If you do not like the color, then you can add a really thin glaze coat of a mid-tone color over the top of everything and that will settle the look down a little. Acrylic paints look lighter and more opaque as they go on but they dry darker.
I seal my rocks with an aerosol matte sealant to ensure that later layers of water-based scenery do not soften them or wash away any of the colors. Alcohol washes can easily be removed if rewet. This also ensures that the rocks are matte as some paints and washes are glossy when dry.
This is just the basic rock painted and now there are a wide range of further details you can add from pigments and stains to moss and lichen.

STEP BY STEP • FINISHING OFF

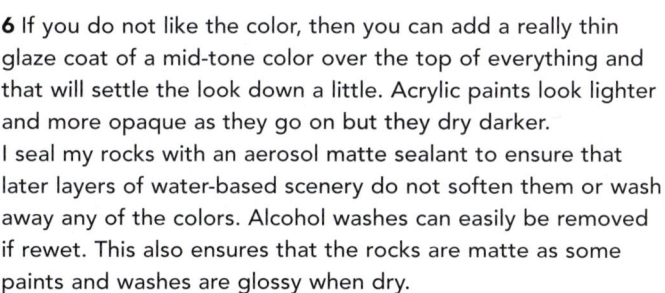

1 When adding the ground layer in this area, I sifted tile grout across the rocks and brushed it off loosely, leaving some on the horizontal surfaces. I then spray with the normal scenery glues that we discuss in that chapter. This helps tone down the rock face and tie it in to the surrounding scenery.

2 I use Woodland Scenics fine ground foam in green blend and earth blend to add some moss to the rock faces. This is glued with the normal scenery process too. I also put some static grass on the rock shelves.

Lou Sassi

CHAPTER SEVEN

Earth, gravel & mud

Lou Sassi uses what he calls "ground goop" to form the base of his landscape and also to model rutted dirt roads. His formula is on page 85.

The earth is a simple layer that sets the base for the scenery. It can be the main feature if exposed, or it can just conceal what lies below. Earth is not just about dry ground though; it can also be used on dirt tracks, gravel roads, or stony ground. This layer acts as the first proper scenic layer and helps add depth to the subsequent vegetation layers. I generally add an earth layer everywhere that is not solid buildings or tarmac roads; I even add it under riverbeds.

Earth

There are two key types of earth layer—those applied dry, and pastes that are applied wet. The choice largely depends on the layer beneath. Adding dry powders to plaster cloth will not cover the multitude of small holes and will allow the powder to escape below. I often use earth pastes on these to cover the holes rather than adding a Sculptamold layer.

All the scenery products I use are water-based so that they can be layered. It is possible to carry on working with subsequent layers before the first is dry and the scenery will dry out with time.

Paint

Most base layers are white, such as Sculptamold or plaster cloth, or brightly colored, such as insulation foam. The first step is normally to paint these with an earth color. If I am using a paste for my earth layer then I sometimes skip this step, but for dry earth methods, it is important that there are no white gaps showing through. This can either be an artists acrylic—I generally use raw umber—or an emulsion/latex paint in a suitable color. I thin the artists acrylic paints with water to avoid leaving brush strokes. You can mix your own custom colors if you want to be prototypical, but I like to choose a stock color so I can easily match it again later. If you do want a custom color, then I recommend using a color match emulsion/latex from a local DIY store.

Texture, large rocks, and stones

There is a danger that our ground can look a little flat, so to avoid that I sometimes texture before the earth, especially if it is going to be grassed later. This can be done in the base layers; for example Sculptamold often looks uneven. The key point to note is the scale of the model. HO scale bumps should not be knee high! I find it useful to keep a scale man (or mini Kathy) around to check that the textures look reasonable. That said, fine vermiculite, ballast, or talus can all be added to give fine texture.

BUILDING A ROCKY SCENE I bedded these rocks down into the Sculptamold base while it was still wet. This acted as a glue and ensured the rocks were part of the base layer. I then added tile grout around them to ensure they were integral to the landscape rather than sitting on top of it.

It is best to glue large items beneath the earth layer such as any large rocks or stones. However, I generally add the smaller ones after the earth layer to avoid burying them. I use a layer of neat white glue and then add the large rocks and stones or texture materials. Disposable foam brushes are very useful for applying white glue and I do wash them out afterward and reuse.

Earth layer

Next is adding the earth layer itself. I generally use tile grout for this. It comes in a variety of colors, from beach sand to dark brown; it is robust when glued as it includes cement, and it is cheap and readily available. It is also a water-based product, so it can be used safely on foam. You can add sand or soil to it to achieve different textures and it is very easy to apply.

If you cannot find the right colored tile grout, then you can either mix a few shades together or paint it after it is dry. The tile grout is very solid and easy to paint with an airbrush or paintbrush. After all the wet scenery is finished, you can come back and add dry pigments or more dry tile grout to add more variety in color to the scene.

Unsanded tile grout, which is the normal dry powder sold in the UK, is hard to glue as it is so fine, so I add one quarter to one third silver sand to allow the glue to penetrate. Without this, the glue often just balls on the surface.

There is a wide range of other products that can be used for earth:

TILE GROUT is very effective when used as the final earth surface to a layout or diorama as here in this road, which is a mix of taupe and beige grouts.

TOP SOIL I used real top soil, as it was dark and rich looking, for this scenic base on a snow diorama. It needs to be well sealed or the color can bleed into the snow, but it is perfect for forest floor. I did not sieve this so that there was a large range of textures and small stones in the soil.

TEXTURE PASTE These small dioramas used texture paste for the mud areas. It was later covered with a wash, then snow.

Soil—I use purchased topsoil for the yard because it is very fine and has quite a lot of sand in it, but not too much organic matter. I find garden soil can be too dark as there is too much organic matter in it. Soil needs to be dried well and sifted. A variety of sieves can produce grades of "rocks" that are great for building up details as well as the finest grade that can be used for earth.

Sand—I do find it too coarse on its own, even for a beach scene in the smaller scales, but it can be mixed in to bring different textures or used as gravel. This is easily found at a garden center and kiln-dried silver or paving sand is the best color and texture.

Real ash—I have collected coal and wood ash for use in my yard areas.

Ground foam—there are many with earth colors that also start building up the start of vegetation and adding variety to the earth tones.

Talc—this can add a very fine texture but will need to be painted.

Commercial scenery products—not just railways but military, wargaming terrain, and diorama suppliers all have a wide range of ready-to-use earth layers including stones and dead leaves.

Ground goop—a home made texture paste (see "Ground goop" on page 85 for more details).

Modeling texture pastes—these need to be spread on and are expensive, but if you only want a small area to show then they may be worthwhile. Earth texture by Vallejo or AK Interactive is an example.

Small rocks and stones

Once the earth layer is in you can add the smaller rocks and stones. I often add these while the earth layer is still dry and not glued so I can blend them all together. The key here is to find the correct size. The use of a scale person is helpful to keep the texture in perspective. I like to build up these textures around the foot of cliffs and rocks or the edge of earth or grass areas. At this point, I also add in any river and stream beds where the base will show. These may be dry gulches or areas I will add resin water to later. The rocks and stones in a river bed do need

COMMERCIAL TALUS Woodland Scenics talus is perfect for the rounded stones found alongside and at the bottom of water courses.

MIXES These rock screes were built up from vermiculite, ballast, and tile grout. The pink streaks were a color within the tile grout and you often find there will be variations when it is applied.

CHINCHILLA DUST This is a gravel parking lot made using chinchilla dust, then painted.

ADAPTING PRODUCTS These were sold as Welsh Slate Ballast and have an interesting mix of colors and shapes.

to be rounded as they will have been smoothed by water.

When adding rocks, start with the larger rocks first, then add progressively smaller ones through the grades to the finest ones. This will allow them to sit properly against each other and look more natural. You may need to glue any large rocks in place first as rocks rarely sit on the surface of the earth and are normally at least partly buried. I use the same wet water and glue mix to fix them in place.

Products that are useful for representing rocks and stones include:

Woodland Scenics talus—I have every grade from fine to extra coarse in neutral or gray, and I generally paint them to match the rest of the scenery with thinned artists acrylic paint.

Model cinders and ballast—these are useful to represent gravel or small rocks.

Coal—you can smash up coal (it is hard work to get it fine) and use it in coaling scenes.

Fine slate chippings—I bought a bag of fine slate chippings from my local garden center. It was the smallest bag they sold, but will still see me through this lifetime. I graded it with various sized sieves and it is excellent for my North Wales slate dock layout or for a quarry scene.

Chinchilla dust—this is a large gravel size in HO but a big bag is relatively cheap from any pet store.

Fine vermiculite—the color is not natural and is also shiny so this will need painting but the surface is a good representation of broken rocks and I use it on mountainsides for rock screes.

Paint and pigments

I often paint scenery to ensure it has realistic variations. This may be as simple as adding a wash to bring out detail, all the way through to a full covering of paint. This helps if you cannot find the right color for your location, and is especially important in water courses with green slime along the edges and in crevices.

Once all the scenery is finished, I come back and add pigments to areas that will be dry and dusty. This pigment layer adds a matte finish. You can add pigments earlier in the scenery process but spraying wet water and glue to fix subsequent layers will generally diminish the effect of any pigments.

Instead, I fix them with a light dusting of isopropyl alcohol spray if I think the area will be touched. You can

TILE GROUT I brushed dry tile grout along the wheel tracks on this earth road to represent drier earth. The glue in the rest of the grout darkens it so I was able to use the same tile grout as the road itself and not glue it.

GLUES & WET WATER

Fixing down the earth layer is our first introduction to scenic glues. You can use the same glue for most dry scenery and it is worth finding a few favorites and stocking up on them.

First up, glue itself will ball on the surface of fine materials, such as grout or ground foam, and can be hard to get to flow. A good soaking of a "wet water" spray will solve this problem. "Wet water" is any water solution with a lower surface tension than water itself; simply put, it flows better.

There are a number of flow aids that can be added to normal water to help improve its ability to spread through the scenery. My favorite is isopropyl alcohol although dishwasher rinse aid, washing-up liquid, polysorbate 20, and commercial flow improvers are all good options.

WET WATER RECIPE
1/3 99 percent isopropyl alcohol
2/3 water

There is a large range of glues that will be suitable but these are my favorites for earth.

- White or PVA glue—this is my favorite glue for almost everything. It is cheap, easily available, cleans up with water and has no noxious fumes. There are some downsides that mean it is not the best glue in every situation. For example, as it dries, it will skin quickly leading to a shorter working time, and it may lose its grip if rewet with later scenery layers. That can also be an advantage in removing or altering scenery later. It will also dry glossy if thickly applied.

- Matte Mod Podge—this includes a sealer, so although it is very similar to white glue, it does not rewet in the same way so it is good to use if multiple scenery layers are planned. It is also matte, which is a real plus point.

- Matte medium—this is found in art shops and adds a matte texture to acrylic paints. It is more expensive than white glue but does not rewet and dries matte.

GLUE RECIPE—DROPPER BOTTLE
1/3 white glue or matte Mod Podge
2/3 water

GLUE RECIPE—SPRAY BOTTLE
1/6 white glue or matte Mod Podge
5/6 water

When using a spray bottle, at the end of every session, you must spray clean water through it instead of glue or the spray head will clog as the glue dries in it.

SPECIAL SITUATIONS

MUD can be created by using any of the earth products with a gloss varnish or some acrylic water products.

REAL SAND is too coarse to use as model sand in HO, but when mixed with a beige tile grout, it creates a perfect beach effect. I used plain sand under the sea, which is made from varnish and water products, to give a deeper color than the lighter mix with tile grout included.

CRACKED EARTH is perfect in areas of quick dried soil and easily modeled with specialist products. Agrellan Earth by Citadel paints was used for this patch of earth. The thickness of the application affects the size of the cracks with thinner layers giving smaller cracks. I have found that these flakes have remained firmly stuck, but if they become loose then a little diluted matte medium can be used to glue them down.

buy commercial pigment fixers that do not tone down the pigments as much.

I sometimes apply heavier pigment coats by creating a "paint" using the dry pigments and isopropyl alcohol mixed to a paint consistency. This is fairly permanent once dry, although you can rub it off if you try.

There are a number of different types of pigments you can use:

Specialist pigments, such as the Mig and AK Interactive brands, come ready ground in handy containers and are very fine. There are a wide range of earth, rust, and green tones but they are expensive to use on large areas.

Chalk pastels—I use artists pastel sticks, which come in a wider range of colors than the specialist pigments. I scrape the side with a craft knife blade to get a fine powder.

Different colored grouts—I love my tile grouts and adding more in a variety of colors can bring back the dusty look.

GROUND GOOP

There are a number of recipes for "ground goop" which is a thick paste that can be used as a very realistic earth layer. This is the classic recipe from Lou Sassi:

- 1 part Activia CelluClay—an instant paper mache product
- 1 part fine vermiculite—a soil additive sold by garden stores
- 1 part earth-colored latex (emulsion) paint
- ¾ part white glue
- Water—add sufficient to make the mix spreadable

Store in an airtight container. Lou also adds Lysol to prevent mold growth while he is storing the wet mix.

STEP BY STEP • EARTH

1 Tile grout, top soil, or any dry earth product can be applied using a sieve. This one is from Precision Ice and Snow and is 700 microns. I started out with a tea strainer sieve, and have also used the popular method of a spray can cap with a pair of tights over the open side. I find this sieve is easier to fill up again. I used fine vermiculite under this section to add some texture.

2 I used wet water and dilute matte Mod Podge to glue the tile grout. See "Glues & wet water" on page 84 for details of these. The trick is to use a fine spray from a distance so as not to disturb the fine grout layer. Too thick a grout layer will prevent the glue from soaking in. Adding sand to grout will help with this, but I apply two thin layers, gluing each in turn, rather than one thick layer. You can add the second layer immediately to save time.

3 Any large stones or thicker patches of grout can be glued with a dropper bottle and a slightly stronger glue mix.

4 You cannot use dry grout over plaster cloth as the holes let the grout fall through. I therefore use a mix of 1 cup water, 1 cup white glue (to prevent cracking), and 2 to 4 cups of tile grout to create a slurry that can be applied with a brush or spatula. This will cover all the holes. I recommend two thin applications. Lou Sassi uses ground goop (see page 85), which has more texture than the tile grout and can be kept wet for longer. The cement in tile grout will cause it to set over a relatively short time.

5 The slurry can dry a little smooth textured, so I add a final coat of tile grout and another light spray of wet water and glue to get the right earth texture.

6 The left hand side was applied dry and the right hand side was applied with a slurry of tile grout first. The final coat in each case was dry tile grout so the finish is similar.

CHAPTER EIGHT

Roads & paths

Dale Latham's HO scale Piedmont Division incorporates well-used back-country roads. *Paul J. Dolkos*

Our layouts are miniature representations of the real world. The first thing you see on most maps is the transportation routes, whether that be rivers, roads, or railroads. As modelers, we concentrate on the railroads, but most buildings or points of interest should also be linked by a road of some sort. Roads are great features to draw viewers into our layouts and are anything but boring.

Geography and people

When planning your road system, the geography of your area will be paramount. Hilly or mountainous areas give opportunities for winding roads and stunning bridges that can be focal points. Flatter areas can still have twists and turns to add interest and make the eye travel farther while viewing them.

Planning roads

Roads are easiest to model on a relatively flat base, so I like to mock in roads at the planning stage. I generally add in the backdrops, scenic contours, and rock faces before adding my road bases and bridge abutments. I then model the earth layer before moving back to my roads. At this point I add in the bridges themselves, sidewalks, any textures such as gravel, and I paint the main colors. I generally finish off the rest of the scenery before adding the final details, such as signs, weathering, and road markings, at the very end. However, if any scenery will make access difficult, then I finish roads before adding in trees and buildings.

There are a number of considerations to bear in mind when modeling roads. First is the width; even single-lane roads are much wider than most of us expect. Traditional town streets were anywhere between 8 and 20 feet wide, but modern cities have tended toward wider streets with 7-foot parking widths and 10- to 12-foot traffic lanes plus sidewalks. That is a minimum of 44 feet, or 6 inches in HO scale, for a city street with side parking. This is much wider than many have room for on a layout, so roads are often subject to selective compression. Fortunately, this is only really noticeable if multiple cars are placed on a road at once.

The next consideration is the height. Most U.S. highways are typically 5 feet higher than the surrounding land to avoid flooding. We should factor in a slightly raised area for our roads to demonstrate this if appropriate in the area we are modeling.

Finally, roads are not flat; most roads will need a crown. This is built in to ensure that rain water flows off a road rather than sitting on it. We should allow a scale 4- to 8-inch height at the road center. Another area to plan for are manhole covers and drains, which need to be set into the surface. Once you get to the detailing stage then it is important to understand the typical sizes of road markings, crossings, etc. The United States Federal Highway Administration has details for common road markings and signs including railroad crossings (mutcd.fhwa.dot.gov/ser-pubs.htm). Since the early 1970s, the U.S. has generally followed the principle that white lines separate traffic flowing in the same direction and yellow lines separate traffic flowing in opposite directions.

Modeling roads

There are two main methods to modeling roads: a flat sheet material, such as card, styrene, or foam, or a plaster-based product. All of them are suitable, but some will better match different types of roads and locations. There are also trade-offs between weight and durability. For example, I like 2mm craft foam, sold for children, due to the texture. It is so easy to trim around track and it just needs gluing and painting, but it is very soft and easily dented. Plaster is a common material but can be heavier and is messier to apply.

Road Widths			
Type of Road	Number of lanes in each direction	Lane Width(s) (feet)	Overall Width (feet)
Single Track	1 lane only	8-9 minimum	8-9
Country road	1 traffic, 1 gravel shoulder	12, 5	34
Main Street	1 traffic, 1 parking, 1 sidewalk	10-12, 7, 5	44-48
Highway (2 lane)	1 left shoulder, 2 traffic, 1 right shoulder, Median	4, 12, 10 (8 in mountains), 50-60 or 10 plus barrier	52 plus median (50 in mountains)
Interstate (4 lane)	1 left shoulder, 4 traffic, 1 right shoulder, Median	10 (8 in mountains), 12, 10 (8 in mountains), 50-60 or 10 plus barrier	64 plus median (60 in mountains)

Older roads and interstates may not meet these modern standards.

● **Types of roads or paths to model**
There are a wide variety of paths and roads from a small footpath to an Interstate highway with everything in between.

FOOTPATHS are everywhere as people and animals take the shortest path to their destination, cutting across corners, wearing down grass and creating tracks. They can add interest to grass areas, as here on a model scene of the Lake District.

DIRT ROADS are a great way to add variety to the roads on your layout as here on Flemming Ørneholm's HO scale Eagle Creek and Northern. *Flemming Ørneholm*

GRAVEL ROADS Bill Iwan modeled these gravel roads on his Red Rock, Green River On30 layout using sifted decomposed granite. *Bill Iwan*

CONCRETE ROADS Howard Clark's layout is an urban scene, so he paid particular attention to modeling the many streets. This is poured plaster that was carved to represent a concrete street with expansion gaps, cracks, weeds, and manhole covers. *Lou Sassi*

ASPHALT ROADS The most common road surface in the U.S. is probably tarmac or asphalt, but, ubiquitous as they are, they do not need to be boring. Pelle Søeborg has added vertical movement to his highway to increase the interest. He also has a dirt track running alongside the railroad. Pelle modeled the highway using the Woodland Scenics paving system. *Pelle Søeborg*

SIDEWALKS Tony Koester has found space to add a variety of different sidewalks, railroad crossings, and a parking lot to his Wingate O scale layout. He used foam to construct the layout and thinner foam sheets glued on top for the roads. He followed this with tile grout on the scenic areas before painting and adding stone dust to the gravel sections *Tony Koester*

COBBLESTONE STREETS Raymond O'Neill has captured a gritty urban feel with his 59th and Rust layout. It includes a variety of street surfaces including cobblestones and inset track. Raymond used a spackle, glue, and paint mix over Wills plastic cobblestone sheet to achieve that inset look. *Raymond O'Neill*

CROSSINGS Brian Wolfe has captured a typical grade crossing scene on his Western Maryland Railway, Blue Ridge Division. It is a scene that is common on almost every layout and details such as signs, lights, and road markings are essential. *Paul J. Dolkos*

MUDDY ROADS The step by step to achieve this detail is later in the chapter, and the puddles are added in the water chapter. They combine to give a very effective muddy road with tire marks and deep ruts.

● Materials

Modelers are spoiled for choices when deciding how to model roads. There are many different road compounds and systems by a variety of manufacturers:

PLASTER is one of the basic methods that is highly successful and can easily produce roads of any length or type. Its surface finish is close in texture to concrete and asphalt and it takes paint easily. I will admit to having a love-hate relationship with plaster though. I used it to embed track in my first U.S.-themed layout and I put the level a little too high. All my steam locomotives' pipework caught on it and some rolling stock derailed. I sanded it for ages, but it was a hard plaster and I created a lot of dust. Thankfully, since then, some great products such as Woodland Scenics paving tape have made the process much easier.

Pelle Søeborg has used it to great effect on his asphalt roads and embedding rails. He used a scraper between the rails that was slightly lower than the rest of the plaster surface, which avoided the issues I had with fouling rolling stock. When embedding rails, remember to leave the track a little proud so you can clean it without affecting your road surface. *Pelle Søeborg*

PRE-PRINTED TARMAC SHEETS are available from a number of manufacturers, such as these paper ones from Metcalfe Models. I sealed the sheets with a spray varnish, but over time, one side has lifted, presumably due to humidity in the air. The main challenge with any sheet product is hiding the joints, which are clearly visible here. I find weeds and dirt are useful to do this, but my main preference is to use these in small areas less than the size of the sheets.

DECALS Lance Mindheim uses homemade decals to model his roads. He first takes photos of the prototype location, then manipulates the images in photo editing software to ensure the road is square and any perspective from the photograph is eliminated. Lance prints these as decals and applies them to the road surface. You can read more on his technique at: mrr.trains.com/how-to/realistic-scenery/2018/08/modeling-realistic-roads-with-decals. *Lance Mindheim*

TEXTURE SPRAY PAINT I used a textured spray paint over styrene (Rust-Oleum Aged Iron for asphalt and Desert Bisque for concrete) on this area. When first sprayed, the asphalt look is perfect for a new road, but I needed a more weathered look, so I added a fine coat of a very dilute tile grout, isopropyl alcohol, and water to weather it.

THIN STYRENE or card is ideal for paving slabs and concrete slabs as Cody Grivno shows on the Keller Brewery rebuild. It is easily scribed to add cracks or concrete pour lines.
William Zuback

GRIT To model my dock with embedded trackwork I used several methods. The first was chinchilla dust glued to styrene (bottom right) but the texture was a little large for HO scale. I then tried carborundum grit, which comes in a range of sizes from 400 grit, which is ideal for Z to N scale modelers, and 220 grit as here in HO scale. I painted and weathered the grit to ensure it was well glued and to add the variations needed in a dock. Using fine sandpaper will give the same effect, since sandpaper is effectively a grit, like carborundum, glued to paper. You can add cracks to sandpaper by crumpling it then straightening before gluing in place.

ERODED COBBLES Cobbles are often covered up with asphalt over time, but if the asphalt has eroded away, the cobbles are visible underneath. I tried to achieve this look using Noch 3D cobblestone path and acrylic plastic putty smoothing the transition to the surrounding asphalt modeled with card as a base. Adding details like this are important to add interest and realism if you have large areas of asphalt, as I do in my dock.

CHINCHILLA AND TEXTURE PAINT This vacant area has two products—chinchilla dust, which is great for gravel roads in HO scale and larger, plus a Tamiya pavement effect texture paint to the right. I find brush-painted texture paints challenging as I tend to leave visible brush strokes, but I thinned the paint until it flowed enough to self level and was pleased with the outcome. I did use masking tape on the edges to get a crisp line, but removed it before the paint set.

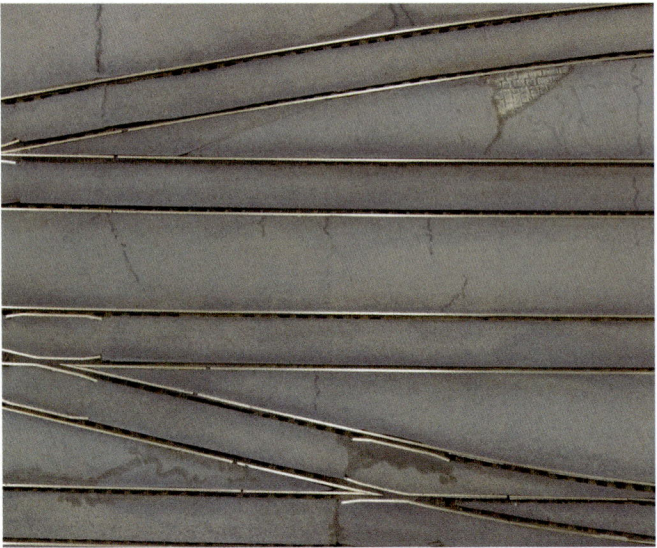

CRAFT FOAM DOCK By far my favorite product for complex trackwork is craft foam. I use the 2mm thick foam sold for children. It is easy to press down onto the rails, which causes a dent in the foam. When you turn it over, you can cut out the exact shape needed. This is good for trackwork, but if you leave a heavy tool on it, it will dent the foam, although it will expand back over time. The texture is perfect for HO scale asphalt.

CRAFT FOAM ROAD I also use 2mm craft foam for roads. It is easy to carve cracks into it, and you can use those cracks to mask the joint between two sheets if needed. Another idea to mask the joints is to use the white lines at junctions.

TILE GROUT It should be no surprise, as it is one of my favorite products, that I also use tile grout for my dirt roads. I normally model these as part of the earth layer, and it is a natural continuation of that. The a step-by-step on the following page shows how to achieve this look.

STEP BY STEP • DIRT ROADS

1 This technique for dirt and gravel roads can be used to model anything from a small footpath up to a country road. This road eventually ends up as a muddy track and you can see how I added puddles in Chapter 10: Water. As a result, the ruts are very deep to ensure that I can add puddles

2 The main ingredient is tile grout, which comes in a range of colors and is readily available from DIY stores, online or from specialist providers. I modeled most of my earth layer on my current layout with the same bag of tile grout so that the colors and textures are similar throughout. Dirt roads should be a similar color to the rest of the exposed earth on the layout.

Tile grout on its own can be difficult to glue as it is a very fine powder and the glue may just ball on the surface. To prevent this I use wet water (see the earth chapter) but adding sand will also help considerably. I normally add a minimum of one third sand, but you could also mix in sieved soil and vary the proportions for different textures.

3 I used Woodland Scenics fine brown ballast at this end of the road to demonstrate a more gravel texture, but you could also use chinchilla dust (bought at pet stores) or any small stone product. Ballast is ideal, but do check prototype photographs as you may need to vary the color from your trackwork as the road gravel may not be from the same source as the tracks next to it.

I tip out a layer, then use a very old brush to spread the ballast directly over my earth layer. The layer needs to be thick enough to hide the soil beneath and allow for ruts to be formed.

STEP BY STEP • DIRT ROADS

4 I use the tile grout mix to create a more dirt-textured road. It is also tipped on, then brushed into the required shape. I form basic ruts in the tile grout mix at this stage.

5 Scale trucks and cars are invaluable in not only ensuring the correct wheel spacing for the ruts, but also in adding texture through tire tracks. If your truck has molded tire treads, then you can also capture that texture too. I wheel my trucks through both the gravel and tile grout areas several times to achieve a well-used look. You can also use the wooden end of the brush to press down the ruts for flatter areas or to form potholes. At this point, all the materials are still dry.

6 Once you are happy with the look of the dry ruts, you need to add a very light coat of the wet water (isopropyl alcohol and water mix—see Chapter 7: Earth) followed by a light coat of diluted glue. To keep the definition in the tire tracks, it is important to use a light spray mist to avoid disturbing the grout, then leave this to dry thoroughly. Once dry, the cement and initial glue will hold the surface of the grout enough that you can spray on much heavier coats of wet water and dilute glue without losing the definition of the tire tread marks. If you want a softer look to the ruts, then you can spray a much heavier first coat which will smooth out the grout as the water settles it in place.

7 Finally, any gravel areas will need a little more glue, so I drip on a dilute glue mix. Once the glue is dry, you can add pastels or more tile grout over the road in the compacted rut areas to give a dusty look. Alternatively, you can brush on a gloss varnish to represent a muddy road or to add a bit of shine to the potholes. I find a thicker varnish such as Tamiya Clear works best. The potholes themselves could be filled with water using resin or an acrylic water product mixed with a mud colored paint. I'll go over this in more detail in Chapter 10.

STEP BY STEP • PLASTER ROADS

1 To demonstrate a plaster road, I created a little section using the techniques. Plaster roads have a great surface texture for painting to create realistic roads and pavements.

2 I used the standard road widths and marked out a city street with two lanes and two parking lanes plus sidewalks. Scale rules make this process much easier.

3 I used the Woodland Scenics roads learning kit for this section. It includes all the necessary products, tools and materials. The technique is to place a 1.5mm foam strip along the sides of the road, then fill it with plaster and use the foam tape as a guide to smooth the top. I started by putting masking tape down to make removal of the foam tape easier as otherwise, I struggled to remove it. The tape is easily applied along the marked edges. Try to keep it as even and straight as possible.

4 The system uses Smooth-it, a thin plaster, for the road surface. You must allow it to stand and absorb all the plaster into the water before stirring or you will get lumps. Stir well but try not to add too many bubbles as they will show later.

5 Pour the plaster into the road and use a straightedge to drag along the surface and smooth the plaster out. I used a ruler as it was wider than my road.

STEP BY STEP • PLASTER ROADS

6 I actually did this in two steps as I found the first pour was a little below the foam tape and there were some holes.

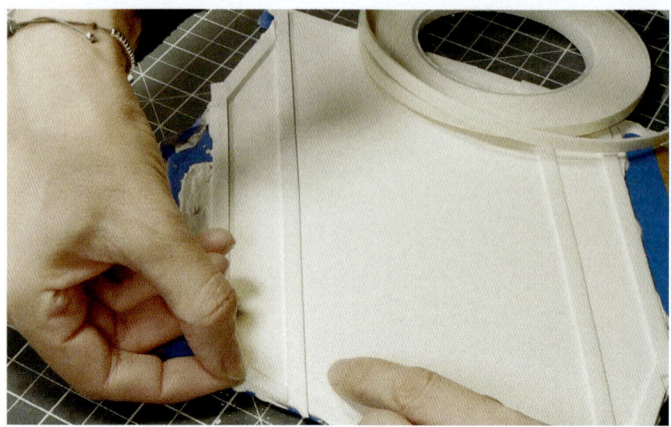

7 Once the plaster is dry, you can add sidewalks using another layer of tape and plaster. You can use masking tape again to make it easier to remove the tape over the plaster.

8 I mixed a small amount of plaster and used the supplied styrene this time to drag the plaster smooth.

9 Removing the tape was difficult until I sprayed the plaster with water. This seeped under the tape and then it released easily when scraped with a knife or pulled with a pair of tweezers.

10 Once fully dry, the plaster needs to be sanded to get a smooth finish.

11 Sanding reveals any hidden bubbles in the plaster. You can fill them, although mine were only on the pavement so I chose to leave them in place.

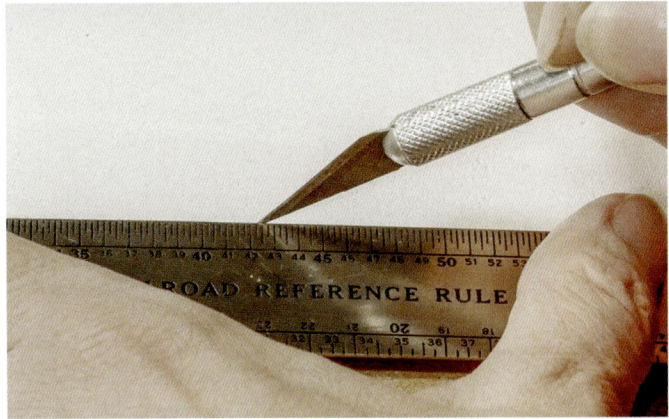

12 I scored in the curb stones and paving slabs or concrete gaps. I use a scale rule and the back of a hobby knife blade as it gives a nice size line.

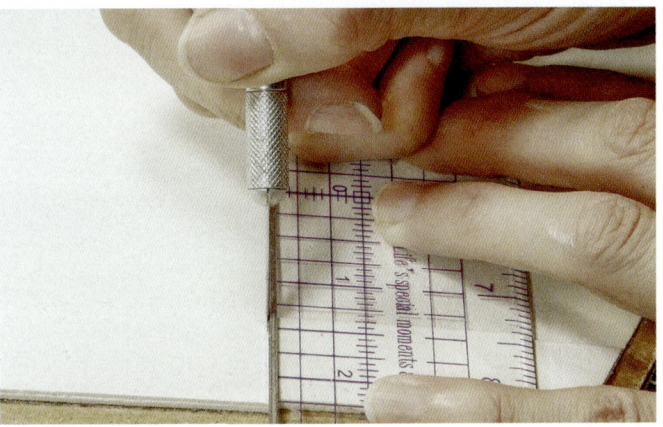

13 A clear acrylic ruler with a metal edge can speed the process as you can see the existing lines. I also scored some lines in the road for an area that has been dug up and replaced.

14 I also scraped out holes to set the manhole covers and drains into the surface of the road so that the tops were level.

15 I diluted artists acrylic paints to color the roads. The main road is warm gray, which looks more realistic than the cooler grays. You need to dilute the paint so the brush strokes do not show but you will need to do at least two coats.

16 I used a natural colored artists acrylic with a touch of the gray added for the concrete pavements, again watered down and two coats. This colors the scored lines more darkly, which is a great effect.

17 The curb stones are a dark granite, so I painted them with a burnt umber color. This was a bit dark, so I put the second coat of the natural color over the top to tone it down.

STEP BY STEP • PLASTER ROADS

18 If you have any grates or drains then do not forget to color the road underneath black.

19 You can paint areas where roadwork has taken place in a darker color or a different tone. I used a darker gray here and also covered a patch with the pavement color for variety.

20 If you have a steady hand, then you can use a brush to paint in the tar lines, but a fine Sharpie will also work with a ruler.

21 For the road markings, I used white artists acrylic paint dabbed on with an old brush between lines of masking tape. I stuck it to my trousers so it lost some of its tackiness. For broken lines, you can use a scale rule to measure out the length. For more complex markings, you can draw them out on masking tape and cut them out with a sharp hobby blade or an electronic cutter.

22 There were loads of road markings for future road works on this stretch so I copied them off Google Maps and painted them in with a fine paint brush.

23 Metal road components often have a metallic sheen. These etched brass manhole covers and grates were painted brown. Once in place, I rubbed them with some dark steel pigment.

24 The edges of roads often have built up dirt and leaves. Here I used a brown pigment along the edges and also down the center of the lanes.

25 Dark pigments are easy to overdo. A large makeup brush is invaluable for adding a fine layer of grime across the road.

ROAD MARKINGS

Road markings are an essential detail to add realism. There are a number of methods you can use as well as the masking tape method shown here:
- Pens sold for the purpose
- Stencils
- Decals
- Cut your own vinyl
- Painting with a steady hand
- Decals

You can show wear by dabbing on a small amount of road color using a sponge and adding pigments afterward.

DETAILS

Details bring roads to life. These are a few suggestions to add to your roads and streets.
- Manhole covers and drain grates—there are a wide range of premade items from photo-etched brass to laser cut in every scale, or you can design and add your own with a 3D print or decal. Do not forget to paint black under any visible grate holes.
- Gravel shoulders using chinchilla dust or ballast
- Tar crack repairs—use a thin black Sharpie or black paint in random crack patterns or use a sharp knife to cut in place and highlight with a wash
- Scrape away or change the density of the asphalt texture in certain areas
- Patched asphalt—paint a section a different color and outline with a thin black Sharpie or black paint
- Pavement/sidewalks—fill any gaps between the sidewalk and the road with acrylic putty
- Road lines and markings (see above)
- Weathering from road usage—a restrained amount of a dark pastel or pigment can achieve this if applied using a large soft brush down the middle of the lanes or alternatively airbrush a darker color
- Oil drips—black Sharpie or gloss black paint
- Potholes—dig out a bit of the surface and fill with a small amount of tile grout or ballast. There is no need to completely fill the hole
- Drive model cars through muddy areas to put in ruts and car tracks. This works well in areas using grout as an earth layer. In larger scales you can even add footprints, animal or hoof marks. The dirt roads step by step shows how to achieve this.
- Root cracks—especially on pavements/sidewalks where ornamental trees raise up the asphalt
- Puddles—use small drips of resin for water and add gloss varnish around the edges to change the color and surface of the road. A dusty texture will turn darker with a gloss varnish, just like the real thing, or you can paint the damp areas with darker road colors
- Model the change of color after rain with damp patches being darker
- Grass or weeds in cracks—use static grass, ground foam, or even laser cut dandelions
- Leaves along the edges—Woodland Scenics earth blend fine turf or chamomile tea leaves work well for this
- Add rubbish and papers. I cut up brightly colored candy wrappers to model modern day rubbish
- Add street details such as road signs, fire hydrants, mailboxes, telephone booths, utility poles, parking meters, street lights, traffic lights, and newspaper stands where appropriate.
- Adding working streetlights and traffic lights can add animation to a street

Pelle Søeborg added a wealth of detail to the roads on his HO Daneville and Donner River layout, from utility poles, traffic lights, road signs and markings, curb paint, advertising signs, and, of course, vehicles. *Pelle Søeborg*

BRIDGES AND TUNNELS

Bridges and tunnels deserve a whole book for themselves (see Jeff Wilson's *Model Railroader's Guide to Bridges & Trestles* from Kalmbach for ideas), but they are a key part of scenery, allowing roads and railroads to move through the contours of our scenery. Whether you choose a solid stone bridge, a spidery trestle, or choose to plunge into a tunnel through a mountain, they can be a key feature of a scene. It is important to factor in the changes in elevation that allow us to give bridges and tunnels a reason to exist. If you have a solid surface on your benchwork, then you can always cut out and drop an area down to allow space for a river or road to pass under the railroad.

Bridges and tunnels are also useful to act as view blocks or entries and exits from scenic areas to storage yards. Whether that is the classic tunnel entrance or something a little more unusual, they are useful elements in most layouts.

KIT-SOURCED Rick Huntrods built this bridge in place using modified Micro Engineering tall steel viaduct kits. The tall spindly supports add a feeling of height to the mountain scene. In the planning chapter, we looked at leading lines; this trestle leads your eye from side to side but the supports take your eye up and down the mountain. *Rick Huntrods*

CUTTING AWAY Pat Gerstle felt his mountain scenery was too flat so he cut away the layout surface, dropping the canyon floor 2 feet to add this trestle and a much-needed feeling of height. *Lou Sassi*

RIVER CROSSINGS
Railroads and rivers are a perfect combination as shown on Doug Tagsold's Terminal of Toledo RR layout. *Doug Tagsold*

DESERT BRIDGES
Even if you model an area of arid scenery, there will still be changes in elevation that can be used to add bridges. Rolf Malmborg added this bridge over a dry creek and gravel road. *Rolf Malmborg*

SCENIC CENTERPIECE Larry Burk's wooden trestle is a beautiful model and deserves a scene of its own. He has cleverly mixed his foreground river with a background picture in this scene which is just over 24 inches deep. *Larry Burk*

SIMPLE SCENE Even simple plate girder bridges can add lots of interest to a scene. The fascia and surrounding scenery drop down below to allow for a road to pass under the railroad on James McNab's Iowa Interstate Grimes Industrial Track. *James McNab*

CHAPTER NINE

Trees, bushes, & grass

Every scene needs plant life—even deserts. In recent years we have been spoiled for choices on scenery products, and you can now buy entire mats of scenery that just need to be glued down to add instant vegetation. The addition of static grass, ground foams, and even individual leaves enables us to model our vegetation more and more accurately.

Adding vegetation brings your scenery alive. Dave Vollmer used several techniques to convey the wooded feeling of central Pennsylvania, including tall SuperTrees in the foreground and less detailed clump foliage trees on the mountaintops. *Dave Vollmer*

107

● This brings the temptation to detail all your layout to an equal level. But detailing the front scenes more than the back ones will add a feeling of depth, and also take less time and money. The viewer will look at the front vegetation first and the less-detailed background trees and bushes will recede, adding to the perceived size of the layout. I therefore like to think of scenery in three sections: foreground, midground, and background. The same techniques can be used for each of them, but I spend the most time and effort on the foreground and look for cheaper, quicker ways to model the remaining areas.

I tend to use taller trees in the front, bearing in mind that a full-grown tree will be much taller than the average house. These trees have visible trunks, bark, and scale leaves with fine detail on the branch structure. As I go toward the middle of the layout, I may use fewer leaves and more ground foam instead. Tree shapes may become more generic, and I try to use bulk-buy trees to save time. By the background, trees generally do not have visible trunks and the leaves are indistinguishable, so I use ground foam instead of scale leaves. This is where the "puffball" tree, a simple generic shape, comes into its own. Forced perspective using trees and bushes can work well, especially when the ground level is rising, for example up a hill, or else the background trees will be hidden by the foreground ones.

Vegetation has other uses too, such as a small wooded area that can be an excellent view block for staging entry points. Ivy or vines are also very useful for hiding flaws in building construction!

Building up layers and textures is key to realistic vegetation. Natural scenes may have multiple layers of grass, broad-leaf short and tall weeds, bushes, and trees. Each tree may have multiple colors of leaves, and a hillside will have subtle differences between the trees. The more layers we can add to a model scene, the more our layouts will look like the real thing.

Materials

We are blessed to live in a time when there is so much choice in scale scenery materials. This can result in too much choice, but it also adds to the final result. I recommend matching the shape of the vegetation to the material used. For example, grass has long thin

VEGETATION HELPS SET THE SCENE Overseas and foreign layouts open up a whole new realm of regional possibilities. Joseph Kreiss' HO Big Island Rail is set a little closer to home in Hawaii. The lush vegetation, sugar cane fields and mill are all distinctive of the area. Joseph made the palm trees by hand using heavy gauge wire and plastic fern material from a local craft store.
Joseph Kreiss

leaves, so is best represented by static grass fibers that mimic this. Broadleaf plants may be best represented in the foreground with scale leaves, but if they are background plants, then ground foam will give a more realistic and cheaper result. Scale leaves can be bought in a huge variety from individual leaves to entire laser cut or etched brass plants.

For large areas, cost can become a real constraint. You can make your own ground foam from upholstery foam, although I have found it to be on a par with coarse commercial foam. In larger scales, I have successfully cut leaves using an electronic cutter, and you can buy leaf punches to punch out leaf shapes from sheets of colored paper or even real leaves. Natural and found materials can make excellent tree armatures and leaves and these are often free.

GLUES

I use the same glues for all my scenery, but for vegetation, I add a few more:

- **Wet water plus diluted white glue or matte Mod Podge** from the Earth chapter is my favorite glue combination for vegetation.
- **Hot glue**—the more I use it, the more I use it. This sticks quickly and the only downsides are the inevitable strings and it will burn you if you put your finger in it. Low temperature glue may be advisable if children are involved.
- **Spray can adhesive**—this is useful for permanently sticking foliage immediately. As time has gone on, I use it less and less because of the overspray and fumes and have moved to using acrylic aerosols such as War World Scenics layering spray instead. I now prefer to use dilute matte Mod Podge where possible and accept I will have to wait up to a day between layers.
- **Layering sprays**—there are a number of spray acrylic or PVA style glues. They have additives that help with vegetation, and they work especially well when gluing multiple layers of scenery as the spray is easy to apply to existing work.
- **Grass glues**—I was a late convert to specialist grass glues, but my white glue did sometimes leave bald patches where it had dried before I applied the grass. Grass glues remain tacky for longer, which is a real advantage when working with grass. Having said that, white glue will work well if that is all you have.
- **Scenic glues**—I normally use white glue or matte Mod Podge, but I have used specialist scenic glues as well. They often are ready-diluted, which is convenient.

TOP TIP—if you are spraying glues from a pump-action bottle, spray clean water through it when you are finished to prevent the inner workings from becoming jammed as the glue dries.

Scenery order

I like to build my scenery in a certain order, but there is no right or wrong way. I find it easy to add later layers over short static grass, but it is hard to glue bushes on top of long static grass as they will be suspended on top of the grass. This means you need to plan in your bush and tree areas before starting any grass. Static grass sticks well, even without glue, to trees and bushes so I leave them off the layout until I have finished the grass areas.

I start with the trees, but I do not permanently attach them, as their size and shade will determine the lower layers of vegetation. They can be made and put aside while other layers of vegetation are put in. This makes adding static grass easier as the trees are not in the way of the applicator. When adding static grass, you may need to protect earlier layers from the glue, especially water or track, as static grass can be hard to remove later. A dampened paper towel makes a good mask.

Once the tree locations are decided, I apply grass and weeds before adding the bushes. Depending on what is under the trees, I will generally add them back at the end, but add some more ground cover to bed them in.

CHILD'S TREE When we look at a child's drawing of a tree, we often see a brown trunk and green leaves. Trees themselves, like most of the real world, are not that simple and trunks can range from white to red with shades of brown, yellow and gray in between. Tree leaves can be anything from green to yellow or red depending on the time of year and species. Photos help create realistic scenes.

Color

I do try to keep a consistent feel to my scenery by using a common color palette. In reality, this means I use the same products for the majority of my landscaping so the scenes tie together. It does not mean you use only the one color of ground foam or grass though. Any foliage in a different texture or color will stand out, allowing us to draw attention to it or to use this to bring the eye to the front of the layout where we can use brighter colors.

Most of us use commercial products and there is a move to provide more and more realistic colors. However, there is such a wide range of colors in nature that manufacturers cannot provide every color needed. I therefore frequently paint my vegetation to get a wider range of colors. This is easier with an airbrush, but dry brushing also works well. Painting can also be used to add a bluer tone to background scenery to help it recede.

SCENIC BREAKS There is a temptation to pack as much as possible into a layout, but giving each scene space will allow the modeling to take center space. The green of vegetation is a restful color and acts as a scenic break between scenes. John M Johnson uses a combination of water and vegetation to ensure his scenes have depth and interest. *John M Johnson*

TREES

● I split my tree construction methods into foreground, midground, and background. You can use the same materials for most trees, but it is worth spending extra care and attention on the foreground trees as they will be most visible.

BEFORE

REALISTIC COLORS BEFORE & AFTER Out-of-the-box commercial trees are sometimes a little bright, but a coat of a spray glue followed by some ground foam will tie them all together into a much more realistic scene. Note the plastic sheeting to protect my printed backdrop while I do the scenery in front of it.

AFTER

SCENERY DEPTH Here are three types of trees using the methods in this chapter. The foreground tree is highly detailed, the midground tree slightly less so, and the background trees are generic shapes less than an inch deep.

FOREGROUND TREES

EXTRA DETAIL There are a number of methods that I use to model foreground trees. It is important to stress that these are mix and match. You can use any of the armatures, such as natural materials, plastic or wire trees, with any of the methods of adding branches and leaves, such as polyfiber, sea foam or static grass.

113

● Armatures

The basic structure of a tree, the trunk and branches, can be made from a wide range of products, such as plastic, wire, and natural materials. The methods used to hand-make some of these types of tree are time consuming, such as twisted wire trees, so I reserve those methods for only a few key trees in the front of a scene. Quicker trees can be made using purchased armatures or natural materials, many of which will look as good when finished.

Examples of natural materials that can be used as basic tree trunk and branch structures:
- Sagebrush
- Sea foam
- Weeds
- Buddleia—especially older plants—makes amazing large trunks for conifers
- Rosemary/Lavender
- Hydrangea
- Roots

I favor twisted wire for those hero trees that will get the most attention as they are unique. Each tree will be individual and you can use photographs of real trees to make the branch structure as realistic as possible. Each species has distinctive branch structures, and using pictures of winter trees will show the basic shape needed. You can also get some excellent plastic armatures ready-made, but I find the price mounts up if you want too many of these in a scene.

Conifers deserve special mention and I model these with a wooden dowel or real wood trunk with wire branches at the very top where the wood becomes too thin to hold the branches.

BUDDLEIA TRUNKS These tall pines were modeled using an old Buddleia bush, which had a perfect bark texture. Holes were drilled and natural twigs from a herbaceous plant were used as branches. Static grass was added for needles. Much of the ground cover is tea leaves, both English and chamomile.

NATURAL TRUNKS Mike Confalone used natural materials for his winter-themed HO Woodsville Terminal RR. These make great bases for foliage or can be used as here for winter trees.
Mike Confalone

● Bark and trunks

Bark is important feature of foreground trees as it will be so visible. There are many ways you can represent bark, and at the very least, a good paint choice will help. Other methods I have used are:
- Latex rubber over wire trees—it remains flexible, which is a benefit if the trees need to be moved
- PVA mixed with a texture such as sawdust, ground foam, or artex
- Celluclay, which is a papier mache product, but can be prone to cracking
- Wrap crepe tissue paper around trunk for realistic wrinkles
- Scrape a dowel or plastic trunk with a saw blade or wire brush to add grooves
- Use a twig of the right shape and bark texture
- Paint with a stiff brush for vertical lines
- 3D printed trunk

Tree trunks can be further detailed with ivy or dead ivy stems wrapped around. You can use bought foliage mats or jute string for dead stems. Consider adding lichen with flicked paint or liquid pigments. I dissolve scrapings from green chalk pastels in isopropyl alcohol to make a thin paint. When it dries, it has a perfect chalky matt finish. You can also add moss using fine ground foam.

CREPE TRUNKS Tree trunks have a variety of textures including ridges, bumps, and peeling bark. I like to represent ridged bark with crepe paper. Here I am using the wet latex applied to a wire tree to glue the crepe in place. First, I cut it to size and then attach one side vertically before wrapping around the trunk.

NATURAL TRUNKS This tree is a simple twig from some garden pruning with polyfiber used for the branches. I sprayed glue, then scattered on some ground foam with a slightly lighter shade at the top. It took a matter of minutes to make and the bark is very effective, but you need to have suitable natural materials at hand.

3D PRINTED TRUNKS 3D printing is a technology that is becoming more and more prevalent in scenery, and I wanted to see if I could use it to make a tree. The branches are just a little too fine to print at the moment, but I was able to design and print a trunk for this winter tree where it will be very visible.

● Branches

Branches are needed to hold the leaves. For really full trees, the easiest method is to add a polyfiber or similar net, finely stretched, over the armature branches. Postiche, a plait of hair used for theatrical use, is a great substitute as well. For winter trees or ones where the branch structure will show, I use two main methods: adding sea foam sprigs (the material SuperTrees are made from) or using static grass to bulk out the armature branches. The latter works especially well on conifers, but can look a little sparse on a large deciduous tree unless there is a very dense wire armature.

● Leaves

Scale leaves add much-needed realism to foreground trees and there are so many different types to buy or make. Leaves can be slightly large as the eye just registers the detail, not the size.

Some are easier to scatter than others. I find the leaves made from paper tend to clump a little, and I struggle to get an even covering unless I shake them out of my grass applicator (without it being turned on). However, a wide range of leaves will add variety and more texture to your vegetation, so it is worth using more than one manufacturers' leaves to get more colors, leaf sizes and shapes.

Here are some suggestions for leaves to create realistic foreground trees:
- Ready bought foliage mat—these are also excellent for bushes as well and can just be stretched over an armature
- Noch or other brands' leaves over polyfiber or static grass branches
- Silver birch or hornbeam catkins for sycamore/maple. The fillers between the seeds are used here. I find drifts on the pavement in the late summer/early autumn and collect them. Once dry they are excellent in larger scales and you can buy these commercially too.
- Moss for conifer branches and needles
- Feathers or electronic/laser cut vinyl and paper for palm leaves
- Fine or coarse ground foam
- Static grass for pine needles
- Scotchbrite pad for conifers

TREES LEAVES There are many manufacturers of leaves and you will need a variety to achieve the different looks in nature. I like to scatter leaves such as Noch or Heki but the other types also allow for larger leaves and a wider range of colors.

Gluing the leaves is very important. I know there are a lot of fans of hairspray, but the brands I have used have not worked and the leaves have often fallen off later. Spray adhesive or matte varnish spray will work, but recently I have moved to diluted matt Mod Podge (1:5 Mod Podge to water), which I find much more house-friendly with no odor, plus it offers water-based clean up.

Once the leaves are glued, I may airbrush lighter colors on the top or use different colored leaves to add more layers of realism. This is especially important if modeling autumn trees where the colors are not uniform in any one tree.

CHOICES It is worth trying a range of manufacturers' leaves over simple armatures to decide which ones you like best. This photo is from many years ago when I was experimenting with the leaves to use for my layout. I finally decided on using predominantly Noch as they scattered very easily and offered a range of colors, including one which suited my location.

SIGNATURE FEATURE Lance Mindheim scratchbuilt these stunning Palmetto trees to add a signature feature to his Los Angeles Junction railway. He used styrene rod for the trunks and cut the fronds out of vinyl using an electronic cutter before painting for additional realism. *Lance Mindheim*

Planting trees

Planting trees is the next step. Trees will normally grow upright, so it is best to have the majority of trees planted dead straight. I add a spike to the bottom by inserting a wire into the trunk base. I drill a hole or, for plastic trunks, heat up a length of stiff wire over a candle and push it in. This melts the plastic and once cool, is very robust. I have started to use hot glue to hold the trees in place as it grabs almost immediately and is very firm but easily removed if needed.

For trees where the ground beneath is visible, it is important to consider what vegetation will be growing below the tree canopy. Dense woodland normally has very little undergrowth and the earth is covered in a layer of leaf mulch. An easy way to represent this is either tea leaves—I favor chamomile as they are lighter in color—or crushed natural leaves. I have a blender I use just for scenery that will grind up the leaves to a range of sizes. You can sieve the blended material to achieve anything from a fine dust to the perfect dead leaf mulch.

Fallen branches, weeds, ferns, grass tufts, and moss are all details that can be added in woodland areas. Single trees or those at the edge of a woodland are more likely to have grass or bushes around them.

Detailing

You can add a lot of variety once you have the key methods. Dead trees can be modeled for effect and are excellent for showing off interesting branch structures. Fallen trees can add variety to a scene.

Some trees are managed by man such as by pollarding (cutting off the central stem or trunk at a desired height), or branches lopped off, and can make interesting shapes or features. Woodlands are tricky and close trees need to merge their branches. I often model these as a group in place with interlocking branches. You can ensure canopies interlock in a single variety woodland if you plant the trees then add the polyfiber base and the leaves.

Different tree varieties have different branch structures and photos of bare winter trees can be invaluable. For example, some trees droop, such as willows, and can be modeled with postiche or polyfiber pulled straight (you may need to wet and hair dry the postiche straight).

You can add further interest with birds' nests or mistletoe. Both are easily modeled from static grass. You will not need an applicator, just form a clump into the right shape. These are especially popular with children (and adults) if birds are also added, such as to an eagle's nest.

For logging areas, stumps can be made from real wood branches, bought castings, or 3D printed. Twigs or dowels can be cut up to represent logged trees.

WIRE TREES Martin Welberg used wire trees and static grass branches to make these stunning silver birch trees. You can see his partly completed trees to the right. Martin used wooden dowels for the trunks before adding wire branches. He uses flexible joint filler for the bark, and adds finer branches from static grass before adding Scenic Express Superleaves. *Martin Welberg*

STEP BY STEP • WIRE TREES

Wire trees take a little more time, but can be used to make special one-of-a-kind trees. These same basic trees can also be used as a basis for a polyfiber tree, or you can add sea foam branches to bulk them out more (see the Polyfiber Trees step by step). Wire trees use a wide range of materials from thin 32 gauge florists' wire, polyfiber, scale leaves, static grass, and coarse ground foam.

1 Start with 8 to 10 pieces of 28 to 32 gauge florists' wire or equivalent. For a tall spindly tree you can use them as they are but for this small tree we will fold them in half.

2 To make a firm trunk, twist the bottom section, allowing enough length for pushing into the ground, and use a pair of pliers to tighten and squash the bottom of the loop.

3 To make a branch, split off three or four wires from the main trunk and twist them together. Once twisted, they will have formed a small side branch. At that point, you further subdivide the wires and twist each of those to form more branches.

4 Once your branch is the required length, fold it back on itself into a loop. Twist the loops to secure them. Here I folded two wires back but sometimes I fold the wires back individually to give a more staggered branch pattern.

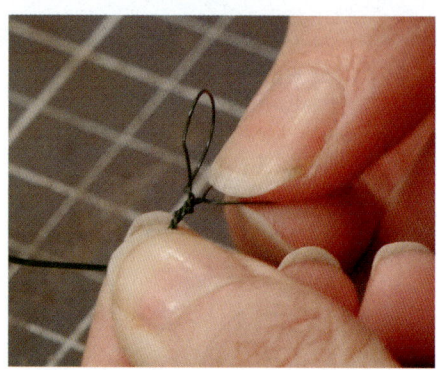

5 Twist each loop individually to secure them. If you do not twist enough then they will fall apart when you snip them later.

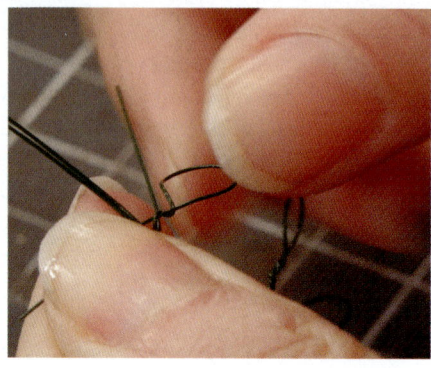

6 Continue up the tree splitting and twisting the wires as you go. When you twist a single loop then leave a tail, as here.

7 Twist this tail into the remaining wires to secure it in place.

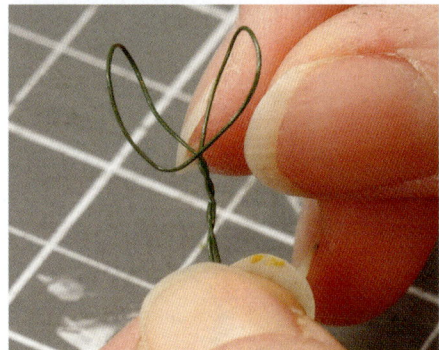

8 Any loops that are too large can be squashed in half and then twisted into two loops.

9 Finally, you need to snip the loops. I like to do this asymmetrically to ensure that they look varied but it does depend on the type of tree that you are modeling.

10 Continue up the tree until all the wires are used up. Twist the main trunk in between the individual branches to ensure that the tree has sufficient height.

11 The wire twists are visible. To cover them you can use a range of products, but my favorite is brushable latex rubber. This is slightly thicker than casting latex, and remains flexible so you can move the branches around later if you need to rearrange them. You need to ensure it dries fully between layers as the outer layers become airtight as they dry, preventing the inner layers from curing properly.

12 One layer is not enough, so I add something like sawdust or fine ground foam to subsequent layers to speed up this part of the process. Brush this second layer on to the bigger branches.

13 I use polystyrene foam from packaging to hold the trees while they are drying as the trunks will push in very easily.

14 When the rubber is dry, it needs painting. If you cannot find a brown colored static grass for the next step, then you can do that step first to ensure that the tree is evenly colored. Acrylic primers are slightly flexible so work well over the rubber. Here I used a brown acrylic primer sprayed from my airbrush.

STEP BY STEP • WIRE TREES

15 Trees are not necessarily brown, so a second coat of paint in a suitable color will be needed.

16 At this point you can add polyfiber (see the Polyfiber Trees step by step) or use static grass as shown here. Spray with a spray glue and cover the edges of all the branches. It is important to avoid the trunk if possible. I prefer an acrylic spray glue because the fumes are not as strong. I also recommend spraying to the side of where you will add any dry items, such as static grass or leaves, so they can be recovered rather than remain stuck to the worktop.

17 Sprinkle on 10 to 12mm static grass from an applicator to add the fine branches. You may need to do this several times, adding more glue and more grass to ensure that you have a full looking tree. The sheet of paper underneath will capture any unused grass and you can tip it back into the container.

18 This is a optional step but saves on leaves and bulks up the tree a little more. Add more glue then sprinkle on coarse ground foam. I use my grass applicator for this as it is handy and gives me a nice fine coat.

19 The very last step is to add more glue and then scale leaves. These are Noch leaves and I find them very easy to sprinkle onto the tree.

20 Large wire trees can be problematic as it becomes hard to twist enough wires together. You can overcome this by creating multiple branches and attaching them to a trunk. I 3D printed the trunk here but other options are to twist multiple bundles of wire together and use a single piece of wire wrapped around to secure them or to use natural trunks made from branches. This is also a good way to pad out shrub prunings if they need finer branches.

STEP BY STEP • POLYFIBER TREES

Polyfiber trees are the simplest way to add bulk to a tree to give full canopies. I used a wire tree armature, polyfiber, ground foam and scale leaves to make this tree. When using polyfiber, you can choose how much of the armature shows through; often trees still show the odd branch, even when full of leaves.

1 I used the same glue for all the layers in this tree. This is an acrylic spray glue and it is important to wear a mask if spraying an aerosol as the fine particulates are not good for your health. I have also used diluted matte Mod Podge in a pump aerosol. Any scenic spray glue should be suitable.

2 When spraying glue, try to avoid the larger branches and just to catch the tips of the branches. I am adding this over a wire armature tree before the static grass branches are added.

3 Stretch out a piece of polyfiber as thinly as possible. I used green polyfiber here, but for my autumn trees I use brown as it matches the foliage color better. Add it in small pieces stretched across the glued area of the tree armature. I tend to glue and add a small piece at a time to avoid the glue drying.

STEP BY STEP • POLYFIBER TREES

4 The polyfiber acts as a base to hold the leaves so it is important to create a full canopy.

5 Each of these subsequent layers needs a good coating of a spray glue. I usually add a layer of coarse ground foam to ensure that the canopy is full. Leaves are more expensive, and padding with a layer of ground foam will also keep the costs down. I am using my static grass applicator as a convenient shaker. I find that coarse ground foam clumps easily and I get a finer application using this as a shaker.

6 I spray more glue, then add a thin layer of scale leaves. These are Noch leaves that I find are easy to shake and do not clump. You do not need to hide all of the ground foam with leaves. The texture and color can add realistic variety to the tree.

7 I recommend sealing the trees if they are to be moved a lot as they leaves can fall off. Dilute matte Mod Podge, or an acrylic matte spray varnish or sealant, both work well to secure the leaves.

8 Commercial foliage comes in a wide range of colors, but you may not always have the exact color you need. I wanted this spring tree to be more yellow in tone than the bright clear green Noch leaves. I airbrushed yellow acrylic paint over the tree to change the tone slightly.

9 Finally, I highlighted the tops of the tree branches with more yellow acrylic paint to add a dappled sunlight look and bring back a bit more variety to the coloring.

STEP BY STEP • CONIFERS

These S scale conifers were made from wood dowels and wire branches. You can buy pine tree kits with the trunk and branches pre-shaped and drilled if you want to short cut those steps. Conifer trees use a few simple products: balsa wood dowels, 28 to 32 gauge florists' wire, latex rubber, static grass, and coarse ground foam.

1 I used 12-inch-long balsa dowels for the trunks. I struggle to carve them easily with a knife, but a motor tool with a sanding drum makes short work of adding a taper to the trunk. I add the top branches by making a miniature wire tree so the trunk should not be sanded to a point as it gets too thin to add branches.

3 The trunk is lacking bark texture. The easiest way to add it is to scrape along the surface with a fine-toothed saw blade. Scraping will leave some fuzzy bits which can be removed by pulling the dowel against a piece of sandpaper.

2 Mounting the trees requires a firm spike on the bottom. I start by drilling a hole in the bottom and also in the top to mount the top wire branches. I use a thick florists wire to add a 2-inch-long spike with 1 inch in the tree and the rest below. I glue it firmly in place with cyanoacrylate adhesive (CA).

4 I create a small tree to sit on the top as the balsa lacks rigidity when too thin. I bend some lengths of wire in half and then twist the bottom and tighten it with a pair of pliers. I bend down the ends of the wire in a tree shape leaving one final piece upright for the top of the tree. I then glue the top in place with CA.
For the smaller trees, the twisted bottom is too big for the trunk so instead I pick a bunch and let one piece of wire stick out beyond the rest, then use CA to glue the remainder together to form the base of the miniature tree before twisting the branches as before.

STEP BY STEP • CONIFERS

5 I use a spike (here, on a drawing compass) to poke a hole in the trunk to put the branches in. I start with single pieces of wire. To save time I tend to pre-cut piles of different length wires.

6 I used white glue, but CA will also work to attach the wires. I push the wire in halfway to the trunk. If you used balsa then this is relatively easy to do by hand. Farther down the tree I add larger branches by folding a piece of wire in half and twisting the bottom tight with a pair of pliers.

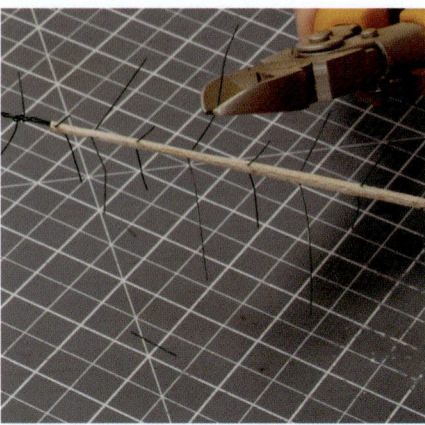

7 When the glue is dry, I trim the branches to a tapering shape. The exact shape will depend on the species of tree you are modeling.

8 The twisted wires will show, so I used brushable latex rubber to add a coat over the top of the bottom of all the branches. I do it to both the twisted and single wire branches to just thicken the base a little.

9 One layer of rubber is not normally enough to fully hide the twists, so I added a second layer of latex with some extra sawdust or ground foam added for bulk.

10 Once the rubber is cured, I paint everything with a brown acrylic paint. Then I spray a fine coat of black to darken the color a little. If you do not have any brown static grass for the next step, then you could paint after that step instead of now.

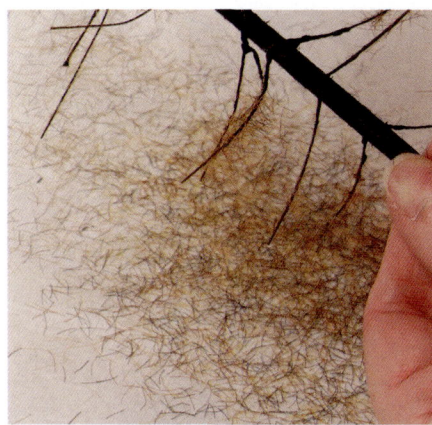 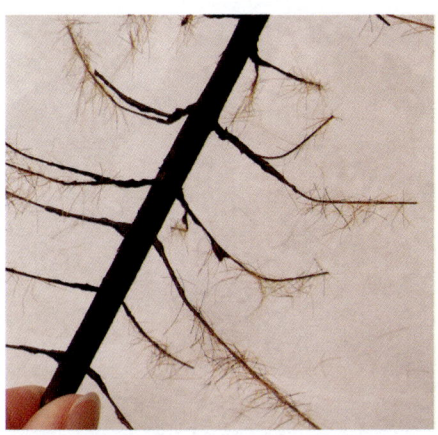 

11 I used pale brown 10mm static grass to add more fine branches to the wires. Start by spraying glue on the ends of the branches, trying to avoid the trunk as we do not want branches there. I use a grass layering spray, but any scenic glue will work.

12 This pine tree has droopy branches, so I used a hair drier to blow the static grass downward. Use a low setting to avoid blowing all the grass off! I repeated the static grass step another two to three times until I had built up enough density on the branches. If you want to model a dead conifer, then you can stop at this point and seal with a matte varnish.

13 like my foliage to be nice and full and with this pine tree, the texture is similar to Woodland Scenics Coarse Foam. Woodland Scenics has a dark green color that is perfect for this. I used my static grass applicator to shake the foam out as I find it gives a much finer application. Again, build up as many layers as you need for a full branch.

14 Finally, I add pine needles using Woodland Scenics Conifer needles (a short static grass). I used the same spray glue and a static grass applicator to apply the needles.

15 The last thing is to clean any excess off the main trunk with a brush.

16 This pine tree was made exactly the same way as the conifers in this step by step, but the trunk and small pieces of branch were left bare at the bottom and the static grass branches were not hair dried downward. I also skipped the coarse foam step as it was not needed.

STEP BY STEP • SEA FOAM

Winter trees benefit from more attention being paid to the structure and branches. This deciduous tree was made with sea foam over a plastic armature. It is a relatively time-consuming method, but gives great results when branches will be on show.

1 Sea foam is a plant that can be bought from many different suppliers with names such as SuperTrees, nature trees, forest in a box, or sea foam. It can be used on its own for small trees and bushes. I find that its trunks are often bent, and my attempts to straighten have often been less than successful. For larger trees, therefore, I prefer to use a more stable base structure and use the sea foam as branches.

2 This is a typical plastic tree armature you will find from many suppliers. You can twist the branches a little and usually you would add polyfiber over the top before adding leaves. This technique would also work very well with twisted wire trees.

3 This step is optional and easily overdone. The branches on this tree were quite straight, and I wanted a more droopy effect, so I waved the tree over a heat gun. This will easily melt the branches to nothing, so keep the tree quite distant and use light quick passes.

4 The sea foam is broken up into smaller branches. Sometimes there are leaves on the plants and these should be removed with a pair of tweezers.

5 I try each branch in place to see where it will fit. The easiest method to glue in place is to use a thick CA that can be set quickly with an accelerator. There are a lot of branches to add, and each one needs to be glued instantly. I dab the end of the sea foam branch in the CA, spray the accelerator on the armature then hold the branch in place. You will need to repeat this many times until the tree is completely covered.

6 When all the branches are in place, I take the tree outside and spray with brown spray paint. This matches the branch color to the trunk and kills any plastic shine from the original armature.

7 This is a winter tree. The same steps would apply to a summer tree, but using leaves instead of snow. I first spray with a dilute mix of dilute matt Mod Podge (1:5 Mod Podge to water).

8 I then sprinkle on the snow or leaves. You will need to build this up in many layers.

9 I recommend turning the tree upside down between layers to ensure that everything is well stuck. With leaves, I finish with a final soaking of dilute matte Mod Podge to make sure the leaves will stay in place.

MIDGROUND TREES

● These are where the vast majority of my trees sit. They are a halfway house between the highly detailed foreground trees and the hardly detailed background trees. For speed and ease, I use ready-made trees, either natural or plastic, and detail them enough to look realistic. This is where bulk production methods and price become very important as there are often large numbers of trees on a layout.

Natural materials can provide some excellent results if you are lucky enough to be able to obtain them in bulk at a reasonable price. Sea foam, goldenrod, sedum, caspia, and many others can be used simply by adding a coat of spray paint, then gluing on ground foam.

I favor commercial bulk trees as I do not have access to reasonably priced natural tree material. These trees are often almost good enough just to go straight on a layout but, in most cases, I will do some quick improvements. The trunks will generally still be visible and that is where bought trees may need additional work. I often add more ground foam to give a denser canopy, but also to tie the trees into my layout color scheme.

There are a number of ways to improve bought products:
- Texture plain trunks either with a textured paint or by scraping with a saw blade
- Use matte varnish or paint on shiny trunks
- Add additional foliage, especially leaves, on top of existing foliage
- Airbrush additional colors, such as lighter colors on top
- Add static grass needles to conifers

BULK FORESTS Tony Koester used sea foam or SuperTrees for his deciduous trees on his Nickel Plate Road St. Louis Division. He estimated it took 60 seconds to make each tree. First Tony prunes the tree to shape, then he sprays with a medium gray primer before using hairspray to glue on Noch leaves. He leaves some trees at the paint stage to represent dead trees.
Tony Koester

STEP BY STEP • IMPROVING COMMERCIAL MIDGROUND TREES

1 These are shop-bought trees that come with ground foam already on them. They look good, but with a few easy steps, they can look great. This is purely optional, but I find it easier to mount trees into finished scenery if they have wire spikes on the end. If you want to leave the roots, you can, but I am planting these on to the sides of hills and the roots will get in the way.

2 Adding spikes to plastic trunks is easy. If your base trees are wood, then you can drill a hole, but with plastic, I do not need to. I heat a piece of stiff wire over a candle flame. While the wire is still hot, I push it vertically into the trunk. It will melt its way in and when it cools, the plastic will hold it securely. The larger trees are often slightly hollow so the wire is easy to push in.

3 I paint the tree trunks using model paints. If you want to add texture, you can drag a fine saw blade or stiff wire brush along first or use a textured paint. Many plastic trees have great texture but are just a bit shiny.

3 Next, I add more leaves to the canopy. First, I use a spray adhesive or spray dilute matt Mod Podge. I sprinkle on ground foam or leaves depending on the effect I am after. These trees are toward the back of my layout and I do not want too much detail on them so I have used fine turf green blend by Woodland Scenics.

4 You can add more glue, then sprinkle on more colors, such as this yellow color to represent a touch of sunlight on the tops of the trees.

131

WIRE PINES Ron Morse used jute twine twisted in a wire, like a bottle brush, to produce these realistic looking pines on his HO scale Forks Creek & Central RR. *Ron Morse*

SETTING A SCENE Tall trees and a dark atmosphere show just how effective good trees are in creating a scene on Ken Kirkwood's HO scale Ma & Pa K Railway. *Ken Kirkwood*

BACKGROUND TREES

TEXTURE We looked at some background trees in 3D Backdrops in Chapter 5. The key point with background trees is putting as much as possible into as little space as possible. We often have very little room for our backgrounds as we have filled our layouts with railroads and structures. One way to overcome this is to use very flat but textured backgrounds. Frequently, the methods used for small background trees can also be used for midground bushes.

FOAM CORE SUPPORT I often use foam core to mount small trees as a backdrop. These trees are a few centimeters, or an inch or two, high at most, and come in bulk bags with a bit of ground foam already applied. I generally add more in my standard layout colors. If the trees have bendy trunks, such as wire, then it is easy to make a small hole with the tip of a pair of tweezers, push the trees in, and bend them upward.

QUICK CONIFERS Conifers can be modeled using skewers with filter or kitchen scrubbing pad materials. These can be cut to circular shapes and pushed onto the skewer before covering with ground foam to give a quick and easy representation of a conifer tree. *Jim Forbes*

PUFFBALLS Sam Swanson used the classic puffball tree for his background hills. These are generally formed by rolling polyfiber into a ball, then covering with ground foam. They can be used to easily fill entire hillsides both cheaply and effectively. He also added further depth to his background hills using foam boards covered with coarse ground foam that sit behind the puffball tree hillsides. *Sam Swanson*

STEP BY STEP • MINIATURE WIRE TREES

1 These are three bases I have used for my background trees. Left, thick jute rope can be used for bushes or background trees. First cut it into tree-sized lengths, then unwind, leaving a small amount of rope to act as a trunk. Finally, spray with glue, then sprinkle on ground foam. I generally hot-glue these in place ensuring that the trunks are not visible.

2 Small wire trees can be made up in bulk then used as background trees. I fold four to six wires in half, then twist them into a simple tree shape, much like method shown for the foreground trees but smaller.

3 You can add static grass or polyfiber to act as a foundation for the ground foam leaves. These trees are made with 6mm static grass to bulk up the branches, then spray painted brown before adding the ground foam. They also make excellent bushes.

4 I painted these twisted wire conifers brown before adding short dark green grass. I later airbrushed the color to subdue it a little. The trunks are not detailed so it is important to plant these close together so that the trunks are not visible.

BUSHES AND SHRUBS

● Once I have planned my trees, I move on to bushes and small shrubs. These are invaluable for adding another layer of scenery both in height and color.

MATERIALS There is a huge range of potential bush materials, from specialist to natural bases, ready to put straight on the layout.

Armature

Bushes and small shrubs share many of the same techniques as trees, so sea foam, natural materials, wire trees and the background tree techniques will all come into play. Besides the techniques already looked at for trees, I also use the following:

- Rubberized horse hair. This divides opinion as it is composed of loops of horse hair in rubber cement. It is torn into clumps, painted, then ground foam or leaves are glued on. I use this to model brambles, which are a common scrub plant in the U.K. and have long arching branches, much like the horse hair. This is certainly an easy to way to produce vast numbers of bushes very quickly with just a spray of glue and sprinkle of ground foam.
- Polyfiber can be stretched to produce anything from a low growing spreading-style shrub to a more puffball style.
- Postiche is a plait of hair designed for theatrical use and it can be teased out instead of polyfiber or "planted" in short lengths to act as the center of a more mounded bush.
- Plumbers' hemp can be used like postiche as the center of a bush.
- Extra height can be added with static grass over any of these, which adds a spiky texture. Alternatively, just create mounds of static grass for low growing bushes.
- Moss or lichen can be also used. If completely covered in leaves, these underpinnings are not visible or alternatively, some mosses make suitable plants in their own right. You can make your own by preserving the natural material in glycerine.
- Commercial bushes—there are a wide range of different commercial offerings that are quick and easy to use. Some are fully detailed with leaves and make excellent foreground bushes.
- Foliage mats are commercial mats of ready-to-plant scenery that you can tear up and just glue down to your layout. They are not cheap, but can give ideas on how to achieve the same look yourself in future.

FRAMING These bushes use the step-by-step techniques shown in this chapter as well as a wide range of bases, ground foams, and leaves. They act as the perfect frame to this section of the layout and add far more interest than a grassy bank or rock face.

- Sponges or kitchen scouring pads can be torn up to create bushes, and are useful for hedgerows where the long thin shape can be cut and covered with leaves and ground foam.

Foliage

I treat bushes like trees with those nearer the front of the layout having leaves while those farther back generally have ground foam foliage.

STEP BY STEP • BUSHES

This is an easy and quick way to make bushes as shown on the central bush in this photo. At its simplest, you add leaves to a base material. It works for a range of bases such as polyfiber, rubberized horsehair, sea foam, or other natural materials. Each have their advantages and can be used to represent different types of bushes. I use polyfiber for more low-growing bushes, and I find rubberized horsehair is best for bushes like brambles that have long arching branches. Natural materials come in a wide variety of shapes, and although they can degrade over time, this moss is from a stock I bought when I started modeling again nearly 20 years ago and it is still flexible.

You can produce masses of these bushes at a time, making them very suitable for covering large areas.

These are the three main types of bases—from left to right, polyfiber, rubberized horsehair, and a natural amazon moss base from a florist supplier.

1 First I prepare the bases. Each has a slightly different process. The easiest is polyfiber; it comes in brown and green from suppliers, and you tear a small piece off and tease it out to the shape you want. You can model low-growing flat shrubs through to rounder taller shrubs by the way you shape the polyfiber in this step. I used double-sided tape to secure it to a base for ease of handling while making the bushes.

2 Rubberized horsehair is also torn off in clumps and then stuck to double-sided tape. The horsehair is formed from loops of hair and when torn there may be overly long hairs that need to be trimmed to a suitable length. The loops can also look less realistic than they should and I snip them to create two arched branches.
Natural materials will follow the same steps as the horsehair. I do find sea foam a bit delicate for double-sided tape, but moss or lichen can easily be stuck down.

3 You can add scale leaves at this point, but I find the bushes look a little bare so I like to use a ground foam first to add a little more bulk to the bushes. First, I spray an even layer of glue. You can use any spray glue, but I like to use an acrylic-based one as the odors are less. Here, I used a layering spray specifically made for adding static grass layers, but any scenery or PVA glue diluted so it can spray through a pump spray bottle will work. I have also used diluted matte Mod Podge successfully.

4 Coarse ground foam gives an open bush structure. I sprinkle it onto the glued branches out of my grass applicator as it is effectively a large container with a sieve.

5 Alternatively, I sprinkle a thin layer of fine ground foam straight from the container. I find this is much easier to sprinkle and gives a much denser-looking final bush.

STEP BY STEP • RUBBERIZED HORSE HAIR

6 I add another layer of spray glue, then sprinkle on scale leaves. I try to match the leaf color to the ground foam. These leaves are some of the larger Selkirk leaves made from a kind of tissue paper. I find they clump easily and I do not achieve the fine application that I can get with a different type of leaf. However, they come in a wide range of colors and sizes and the clumps look realistic.

7 These are the finer Heki leaves, and they sprinkle on easily over a coat of spray glue. I do turn these upside down to recover the excess leaves if I have been a little heavy handed, but I find the coarser foams and leaves are more likely to fall off if I do this before the glue has dried.

8 At this point you should add a matte sealant spray to ensure that everything is stuck. I either use a hobby sealer by Plastikote or dilute matte Mod Podge. A good soaking will ensure that the bushes are longer lasting and the leaves remain stuck.

STEP BY STEP • PLUMBERS' HEMP AND POSTICHE BUSHES

I have used static grass as branches on wire trees and you can also do the same for bushes. This technique can produce anything from small low-growing bushes to larger bushes depending on the length of the initial fibers used.

1 Plumbers' hemp and postiche both have long fibers that can be cut to varying lengths. Plumbers' hemp is a bit stiffer and is my favorite of the two because you can make taller bushes.

2 I start by cutting the hemp or postiche to length. They both come in long hanks and are easily cut to size with a pair of scissors.

3 These are best made in batches. I split the lengths up into smaller bunches of fibers. These make up the core of the bush, so can be as few or as many as you want. I pick different amounts for variety. I used hot glue to stick the bunches as it sets very quickly, but you will need to snip the bases of the clumps with a pair of scissors to remove them. Double-sided tape is an alternative if you wish to be able to tear them off.

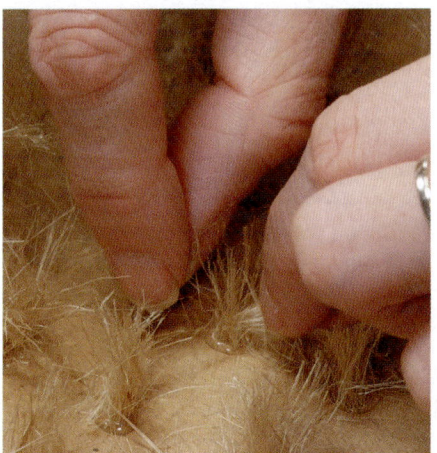

4 I push each bunch upright into the hot glue and wait for it to set. You can leave the bunches as they are, but I like to open them out a bit by teasing the top of the bunch apart. Postiche is treated in exactly the same way, but it is softer so will not stand as upright as the plumbers' hemp.

5 I paint my plumbers' hemp as it is such a light color. You can use any brown spray paint, such as airbrushed acrylic paint or a spray-can paint.

STEP BY STEP • PLUMBERS' HEMP AND POSTICHE BUSHES

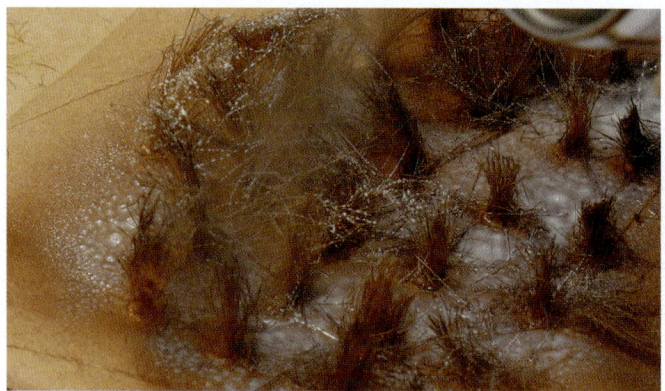

6 At this point, all the bases need bulking out. I add branches using static grass. First, I apply spray glue, such as a layering spray here, a dilute PVA, scenery glue, or dilute matte Mod Podge. I prefer a stronger glue so the grass sticks quickly and remains in position.

7 I use a static grass applicator to apply a layer of 6mm grass. I try to stick to muted brownish tones to avoid painting again.

8 I spray another layer of glue and add 2mm grass. This was green as it was all I had. The choice of grass color can make interesting variations to the final bushes.

9 To bulk the bushes out further, I add a layer of ground foam. I use fine Woodland Scenics ground foam as the static grass branches are very fine too.

10 Finally, I add another coat of spray glue, then sprinkle on some scale leaves. These are Noch leaves on the longer hemp bases.

11 Different combinations of static grass lengths and colors, ground foam, and leaves give different effects, such as these Heki leaves over a burnt grass ground foam.

12 The final step is to coat the bushes with a matte sealant spray, such as hobby sealer from Plastikote or dilute matte Mod Podge.

STEP BY STEP • STATIC GRASS BUSHES

1 For smaller bushes, I use static grass instead of plumbers' hemp or postiche. I start by using grass glue to create clumps of 10 to 12mm static grass. These release well off a sheet of plastic, from a bag for example, or thick foil, which also conducts the static charge. I dab on glue in rows to hold the static grass.

2 I then apply three coats of 10 to 12mm brown static grass from an applicator. If you do not have brown, then you can paint the grass later. I find with one application there is not enough static grass stuck, so I keep applying it, turning the sheet upside down and shaking off the excess grass, then reapplying until I have a reasonable-sized grass tuft.

3 This is how big I make these bushes. I leave them for the glue to set before moving on to step 6 in Plumbers' Hemp and Postiche Bushes, on the opposite page.

4 The bushes made from only static grass are far smaller, but the effect is similar. To tear these off I use a pair of tweezers from underneath to avoid crushing the branches, then plant as drifts of low-lying shrubs. The larger clumps in hot glue were cut off with a pair of scissors.

MIXED TECHNIQUES Techniques can be combined as with these gorse bushes, which layer static grass over polyfiber. The leaves are brown ground foam airbrushed green on the tips. At the right time of year, bright yellow flowers can be seen, which could easily be achieved with a small sprinkling of a yellow ground foam.

STATIC GRASS INSPIRATION Martin Welberg has inspired me with his use of static grass to add bulk to bushes. He uses a wide variety of ground foams and leaves to ensure that his hillsides have character. *Martin Welberg*

SIMPLE AND EASY Dick Christianson used Woodland Scenics' clump foliage to represent the bushes on his Salt Lake Route. This shows that simple and easy vegetation can be very effective. *Dick Christianson*

WIRE BUSHES Ken Patterson used modified Bachmann SceneScape branches to create the low brush alongside this stretch of track. The ready-made wire armatures considerably speed up his modeling process. *Ken Patterson*

GRASS

● I favor static grass to model grass as it has the closest shape of any of the available materials. It is easy to layer to get realistic effects, and I frequently paint my grass to add even more depth.

Firstly, what is static grass? It is colored fibers ranging from 1mm to more than 12mm that will stand upright with a static charge and can be glued in that position.

Static grass is much simpler to use than the science behind it. You simply apply glue to your ground layer, shake on static grass from applicator or puffer bottle, and remove the excess. You may repeat with different colors and lengths for various effects.

There is a huge variety of colors now with more and more ranges being introduced every year. If the color you want is not available, you can mix colors together to get a blended effect, or paint the grass using an airbrush or drybrushing. I like starting with a shorter green layer, then adding a longer straw-colored layer over the top to represent summer grass. You can use any combination of different colored layers or mix grass in the applicator to get realistic effects. I particularly like the dead colors that have been launched over the last few years.

LIFE AMONG THE TRACKS A mix of grass and weeds brings life to the trackwork on Raymond O'Neill's urban layout, 59th and Rust. Grass on track is easily applied using the methods in this chapter or using commercial tufts, but do allow clearance for lighter rolling stock to run as static grass is quite springy. Keeping flangeways clear is also best. I also recommend adding ballast first as the grass is springy enough to stop ballast sitting properly. *Raymond O'Neill*

PUFFER BOTTLE I started with a simple puffer bottle before spending the money on an electronic applicator. It is a nylon bottle with a removable top. The puffer bottle is very cheap, very easy to use and works well on short lengths of grass fiber. You need to fill the bottle less than half full, shake to apply the static charge, then puff onto a glued area from  about 2 inches above the surface. They do not work with large volumes, so you should only glue relatively small areas of a few square inches at a time. Larger areas soon get tiring. They do get into corners easily though, and are good for adding small grass tufts.

If your grass is not standing as upright as you would like, then a quick vacuum will pull it more upright. If you place a pair of tights over the end of the vacuum nozzle, you can collect any unstuck grass to reuse it. You can also fill a couple of bottles with different length grasses and apply them both while the glue is still sticky.

ELECTRONIC APPLICATORS Electronic static grass applicators provide a stronger static charge, meaning longer fibers can be used, and they can cover large areas quickly. You touch the grounding wire near the area being covered to help with the static charge and shake the applicator over the area you want the grass to grow. I try to match the size of the glued area to  the capacity of the applicator so the glue is fresh when I am applying it. I always fill my applicator about half full so the grass can get a good charge. I fill it before I apply the glue so the glue does not dry before I get there.

If you find your grass is clumping into balls in the applicator, then you need to pull them apart. I do this by hand but I hear that some people whizz them up in a blender (I have one dedicated to scenery).

Homemade or cheap commercial applicators are not always as strong and not always as well protected, so do not touch them or you may get a large zap. The better applicators have a range of meshes. You can use finer ones to stop shorter grass flooding out too quickly. Another good tip to stop this is to hold the applicator at a shallow angle when shaking.

PUFFER OR ELECTRONIC The smaller patch of paler grass to the left was done using a puffer bottle, whereas the rest of the grass was applied with an electronic applicator. The grass around the edges is not as vertical on the puffer bottle section, but the result is still more than acceptable and better than just dropping grass on.

● Other grass products

There are a wide variety of other methods for representing grass beside static grass. Fake fur, carpet underlay, medical lint, and heat-shrink vinyl grass mat have all been used to represent grass. Today, there is also a wide range of commercial grass mats, some including highly detailed scenes, such as alpine meadows.

FAKE FUR Gerry Leone used fake fur to represent grass near his town of Eureka on the Bona Vista Railroad. Gerry used green-colored fur, but colors are limited so you may need to brush-paint, airbrush, or dye the fur first. As well as painting, Gerry also trims and brushes his fur to get a realistic effect. *Gerry Leone*

STEP BY STEP • BASIC GRASS METHOD

● This basic grass method will give an even coverage, akin to a putting green in shorter lengths.

1 I used normal white glue for years, but as it dries, it forms a skin. This means it will not remain tacky for long, especially in warmer climates. This can lead to bald spots in the grass, which are not ideal. Specialist static grass glues will remain tacky for longer, allowing you to do larger areas, but regardless, you will need to glue relatively smaller areas in hotter, drier conditions where your glue will dry more quickly.

Spread the glue thinly, or the grass will fall over and not be held upright as it dries. I use disposable brushes to apply the glue, but wash them out and reuse them.

2 An electronic applicator needs to be held just above the glued surface and gently shaken. The mesh should be appropriate to the length of grass fiber, with shorter lengths needing finer meshes. If the grass comes out too quickly, then hold the applicator at an angle.

You will need to hold the grounding wire in the glue or near the area being grassed to pass a strong positive charge to the ground, which will help the grass stand more upright.

Continue applying grass until you get a good coverage. The grass stands upright by repelling the ground and its neighbors.

STEP BY STEP • MIXED GRASS METHOD

● A step up from the basic method is to mix a range of colors in the applicator and apply them all at once.

1 I used a spray scenery glue because the base layer would be difficult to brush glue over as it has a lot of texture. This is thinner but it still grabs the grass and holds it upright.

2 I put a mix of 2mm to 3mm and 6mm grasses in the applicator. I applied the grass as in the basic method, but used a fairly large mesh to allow the longer grass fibers to come out. The shorter fibers will fall through first and generally coat the surface, so continue to shake until all the grass is used.

3 The end result is a mix of short and long fibers. A mix of different colors will give a more marked effect than the same color in different lengths.
This was applied over a very textured surface from the earth chapter, which gives realistic grass humps.

4 Remove excess grass to not only tidy up the work, but also to reuse it. I often work on dioramas, which I can shake onto a piece of paper, then put the fibers back in the packet. If I am working on a fixed piece, then I use my vacuum cleaner with a pair of tights (panty hose) over the end to catch the grass. I also have a dedicated hand-held vacuum cleaner I use just for scenery so I can recover the grass from its bag too if grassing large areas. If you are struggling to get longer grass fibers to stand upright then this vacuum step will also pull the grass vertical again.

5 I often finish with a light spray of a matte sealant since static grass has a sheen to it. The spray will remove this, but test a piece first to ensure that it your product does not create small balls instead of an even covering.

STEP BY STEP • LAYERED GRASS METHOD 1

● There are two methods to add more layers to static grass. This method uses different-length grasses in different locations with shorter grass applied first around the edge of the longer grass patch.

1 Start by adding a layer of short grass around the area you intend to add longer grass using the basic method. Long grass patches normally have a transition through shorter grass before reaching bare soil.

2 Apply the edge grass. In this case I used 2.5mm green fibers to represent the shorter newer grass growth. Tip off or vacuum the excess grass.

3 Apply glue into the sections where the longer grass would be growing. It does not matter if you get a little glue on the existing grass.

4 Add the longer grass, here a 6mm dead-colored grass fiber. This can be as sparse or dense as you need your longer grass to appear.

5 Longer grass fibers often give a less dense covering than shorter fibers as the first fibers obstruct later grass from reaching the glue. I therefore like to go over the area again with the shorter grass fibers from the first steps. This fills in all the gaps and prevents too much of the earth layer showing through.

6 The final result still shows a little of the earth layer through and looks less luxuriant than the next method.

STEP BY STEP • MIXED GRASS METHOD 2

● This is my preferred method as it gives better coverage of the ground layer than the first method. The first layer is a shorter grass fiber, which gives a denser layer than the longer grasses, so when it is used first it completely covers the ground. A second layer is then added using a spray glue to attach it. More layers can be added to get the desired look. There are commercial layering sprays, but I have also used general scenery spray glues and even diluted matte Mod Podge to achieve the same effect. I find that permanent spray adhesives can leave little balls, so you will need to use a glue that dries flat.

If you have had problems with your grass looking a bit sparse then this could be the solution.

1 Apply the shorter grass as in the basic method. I used 2.5mm grass here in a brighter green. Next is adding a spray glue for a second layer of grass. I used a commercial scenery spray glue. There are many brands that offer layering or scenery sprays specifically aimed at adding scenery layers. The important point is that the normal permanent spray adhesives that are used for paper or other crafts may leave little balls rather than a nice thin layer of glue.
Spray the glue into the center of the grass leaving some shorter grass around the edges. You can mask off areas to avoid gluing them or even use a sheet of paper with holes ripped in it for a more precise application of glue.

2 Add a longer grass fiber, ideally in a different color; this is 6mm. Generally, this works well with a dead colored grass over a green or brown base, but you can also use two colors of green. Remove the excess by turning upside down or vacuuming.

3 The final result here is a green underlayer that is shorter and more visible toward the edges. The amount of grass added in the second layer can give a variety of different effects. Subsequent layers of different lengths and colors can be added to give even more variety to the scene. I have also knocked this around a bit (see special techniques).

SPECIAL TECHNIQUES

● These basic methods are only the first steps and there are many more techniques you can use to improve your grass. I often paint my grass, firstly to remove the slight glossy sheen the fibers have, but also to add variety to the colors.

You can trim your grass if it looks too long in places with a pair of small scissors or use them to add choppy variety to areas of long grass.

WINDSWEPT Using a hair dryer while the glue is still wet can give a wind-swept look to longer static grass. The heat will set the glue quickly, holding the grass in the new direction. This is very useful on the sides of embankments where the static grass will stand away from the ground at a right angle. In reality, grass grows more upright, and the hair dryer can be used to set the grass into a more realistic direction.

KNOCKED ABOUT Knock the grass around a bit with a brush end to stop it looking like an even fur coat. I went over this again with some shorter green grass where I had exposed the still-wet glue.

HIDDEN TEXTURE Ground foam, from fine to coarse, or small stones can be used to add bumps and color under the grass and can add some much needed realistic texture to large flat areas.

This overhead view of all the step by step grass methods shows that the bottom area, with vermiculite added under the earth layer, gives a very different effect to the knocked grass (top left) or windswept (top right) finishes.

DIRT AT THE EDGES Adding more of the earth layer, here tile grout, into the grass can help the edges look more realistic as the grout dulls any shiny patches of glue and the sheen on the grass, plus makes the grass look more sparse and worn at the path edges. This is also an excellent way of ensuring commercial grass mats sit in the scenery rather than looking like they are placed on top.

VISIBLE TEXTURE Small stones and gravel—especially around edges—and twigs or junk piles can add much-needed texture to a grassy area. These stones were added as part of the ground layer and the glue carefully applied around them to ensure no grass stuck where it would not normally grow.

MIXING IN GROUND FOAM Consider adding ground foam to add different broadleaf texture or as drifts of flowers. I used Woodland Scenics snow to add white cotton tops to these reeds. You can add drifts of flowers to grass by wiping a finger with diluted white glue across the tips of the grass before applying colored ground foam. A spray of wet water and dilute glue will keep the foam in place.

VACUUM UP Long grass can often fall a little flat, especially with weaker applicators. Vacuuming the grass before the glue dries will drag it back upright again

PAINT FOR PERFECT COLOR I often paint my grass to get the exact color I want. Here I was fading the grass toward the rear to give some forced color perspective to the scene.

DRYBRUSH DETAILS I like to drybrush the dead top grass onto shorter grass layers. I often find that the dead grass fibers are a little dark compared to the colors I want, so I drybrush the tips of those layers too.

GRASS TUFTS

● Grass tufts are incredibly useful and appear in all my scenery. I use the larger ones as clumps of tall grass or reeds and smaller ones around the edge of buildings. You can buy commercial tufts or make your own. I use both, but like to have a supply of commercial tufts in a range of colors and sizes on hand.

WIDE RANGE There is a huge range of available grass tufts and they will suit many different applications depending on size and fiber length.

FLOWER OPTIONS Commercial grass tufts come with a range of flower colors too. They are typically ground foam applied to a grass tuft and are a handy way of adding flowers to a scene.

BETTER SHAPES I usually tear my larger tufts apart to ensure that they do not look too round when applied. This has the bonus of making the tufts go further.

DRYBRUSH ON TUFTS TOO I often repaint at least the tips of my tufts to ensure that there is some natural variation. In this case I was modeling February and the ends of the reeds were pale, dead colored.

BLENDING IN Grass tufts often need to have a layer of shorter grass added around them, much like with a grass mat, or they can look unreal in an otherwise short grass area.

TUFTS FOR REEDS Grass can also be used to model reeds. I use a commercial reeds product for variety as well as larger commercial grass tufts. I find commercial products such as Busch or Noch reeds taper to a realistic wispy end.

This is a very long product and needs to be trimmed to size before being glued in place. I use the lower section farther back in the layout as the ends look too blunt to be realistic in the foreground. This product will need cutting and gluing in place one clump at a time, so commercial grass tufts can be quicker if a large area needs to be covered.

STEP BY STEP • GRASS TUFTS

● Handy as commercial tufts are, it is also easy to make your own. Here is how I make tufts for later use, but you can also use the same method to add tufts in situ on a layout. I find these invaluable to add small patches of grass to all my scenes.

This method is for the most basic grass tufts, but you can also use multiple colors and lengths of fiber to achieve different effects.

1 Using a sheet of foil, add some small random patches of grass glue.

2 Add grass using a static applicator, holding the ground wire to the foil. You can mix multiple lengths and colors or just do one color as here. Do not forget to tip the excess grass back into a container to reuse it.

3 Once the glue is dry, the tufts are easily peeled off the foil and can be attached anywhere with a small spot of glue.

4 You can add tufts in situ by just adding small spots of glue to your layout scene. This is a great way to add patchy grass along cracks or at the edge of larger areas of grass.

WEEDS AND GROUND COVER

● Weeds and broad-leaf plants grow everywhere and I use them in all my scenery, whether city or rural. Along with grass tufts, they are a ubiquitous sight and can add another layer of detail to a scene.

Ground cover is a catch-all description of those areas that have drifts of leaves, rich soil, or dead plants. The vegetation layers we have added often need tying together; weeds and ground cover are the perfect final step to do this.

The simplest vegetation can be a spray of a green, white, or yellow chalky matte paint to represent lichen and moss. Slightly larger weeds can be represented by a dab of white glue and a sprinkle of ground foam. Vertical slopes or hard-to-reach areas can be covered with spray glue, then the ground foam or leaves whisked on. Whisking is where the scenic material is blown over the glue. Using a straw can help.

Larger weeds have even more options:
- Ground foam or leaves sprinkled over grass can give a different texture and the effect of drifts of weeds. Flower colors can be used if appropriate. I use Woodland Scenics snow to represent white flowers.
- Clump ground foam can be bought and used straight from the packet in a variety of different sizes.
- A thin layer of polyfiber can be stretched very thinly to add more height over grass or earth, then covered with leaves or ground foam in the same way bushes are made.
- Reeds/field grass materials can be dipped in glue and sprinkled with ground foam or leaves to act as taller weeds with a central stalk.
- Bulrushes can be made from the same reed material or thin wire but with a brown paint and glue mix painted on the top to represent the seeds.
- Moss and lichen can be preserved in glycerine and used to add very detailed natural plants to a scene. They can be spray painted afterward if the color needs adjusting.
- Laser-cut plants have become very prevalent in recent years with everything from dandelions and nettles to garden plants and vegetables. The plant is printed on paper and then laser cut so it can be removed, twisted and planted straight away. Some plants are printed on white paper and can benefit from coloring the white edges with a felt tip pen.
- Photo-etched brass ferns and other plants are excellent to add small details. These are the predecessor to the laser cut plants and can be a little pricy in large areas. They will also need painting. They can be bought or, if you are brave, etched yourself.
- 3D printing is just beginning to take off and more and more details will become available over time.
- Electronic cutters such as the Cricut or Brother Scanncut can be used to cut out leaves, although I have only found them to be practical in larger scales.
- Leaf punches can be used on colored paper or real leaves. These are also better in the larger scales.
- Plastic florists' materials such as ferns can also be used in the larger scales.
- Vines can be purchased or you can make your own using thin lines of glue on a building with leaves sprinkled or whisked on.
- Jute string is great for adding to tree trunks as dead ivy roots or as hanging vines.
- Cactus can be bought or 3D printed if appropriate for your area.

CUT PAPER FERNS This large scale scene uses a variety of ferns cut on a Brother Scanncut machine and mounted on magnet wire as well as ground foam to represent moss. The vines are made from twisted jute string. These techniques would be hard to do well in smaller scales but in garden scale, they would be very achievable.

GROUND FOAM FLOWERS I used Woodland Scenics coarse ground foam and snow to create this drift of flowers in a grassy area.

COTTON PLANTS Fields and crops often have specific patterns, such as this field of cotton plants growing in straight lines. Steven Otte sprinkled ground foam onto stretched lengths of brown cotton thread to represent this field and the technique could be used for a wide range of crops. *Steven Otte*

JUTE ROOTS This stream edge uses jute string to represent roots and branches with a commercial foliage mat as ivy.

SOFTENING EDGES My final step for vegetation is to look for any gaps around buildings, areas where dead leaves would accumulate, and harsh transitions between scenes. I use ground cover to soften these areas and add more life. My favorite ingredient is a sprinkle of Woodland Scenics Fine Turf in either earth or green blend mixed with ground up leaves (I have a separate blender) and tea leaves, such as chamomile. This mix can be spread around buildings as here, at the edges of vegetation, in gutters of roads, and under trees.

I used scale leaves, applied over thin lines of white glue to hide a broken wall piece in this set of buildings. The bushes to the right are commercial and are an easy way to add greenery to an urban scene.

CHAPTER TEN

Modeling water

Water makes up 71 percent of the earth's surface so it is no surprise that it is a key feature in our model railroads too.

Planning for water

Whether your railroad is set on the coast, one of the Great Lakes, or an arid desert, water will make its impact felt; even deserts have dry water courses. Water itself comes in many forms from a small puddle to a muddy swamp or a raging sea. Each has its own challenges to model, and water needs to be planned in at the opening stages of a layout to ensure it fits in the landscape. It is rare to see lakes at the top of a hill, for example.

Modeling water often scares people, and when you have watched your carefully poured resin river flood out through an unseen hole onto the surfaces below, you can be a little wary of trying the same methods again. However, all that hard-learned experience is in this chapter to prevent you from making the same mistakes.

There are so many materials on the market now to make water that it can be very confusing. I am often asked what I think of a certain product and nine times out of ten, I have not tried it because I have something similar that I know works. An obvious choice seems to be using real water, but I find it just looks wrong as water does not seem to scale down to the right sized ripples or waves.

There are two main ways to model water. The first to model the shape of the water, flat or with ripples, to

The sea is captivating to model, and rail-marine operations add a lot of interest to a layout. This classic scene is based on the Rocky Neck State Park where the New Haven main line runs alongside the beach.

paint it and then to add a gloss coat to give the necessary shine. The second method is to model the surface under the water and add a clear product such as resin before adding ripples and waves. This latter method gives more depth, but the choice will often fall to whether you need the river or lake bed to show or not.

The main decision is what type of water you are modeling and what is the simplest way to represent it in scale form. Moving water requires a different set of techniques than a flat, calm lake. Waterfalls or weirs need to have a change in height to account for

WHAT COLOR IS THE SEA? There is a temptation to look at water and presume it is blue. This scene from South Wales shows the difference that sunshine and clouds, the lighter and darker parts of the sea respectively, make to the color of water. Only the very distant water starts to take on a blue tone with the foreground colors being predominantly grays, often with a green tint. The high tide line can also be seen on the rocks with the lower areas taking on a darker wet color and the colors and tones changing in bands as the tidal range affects the rocks. The high tide line is often marked with detritus such as seaweed and driftwood.

the water moving, and this needs to be planned right from the outset.

You also need to think about the order of adding water into the scenery. For example, I like to pour resin early as it can creep into the earth and grass. If you pour it early, you can easily cover this creep before the main scenery goes in. However, resin can also scratch, so if you are not doing ripples, you need to protect it well for a mirror surface. My preferred order is therefore modeling the scenic base with the earth layer and flat areas for water before adding resin and waterfalls if those are used. I come back more or less at the end to add in the final gloss layer and ripples. If the water has dulled during the scenery process, then I use a layer of gloss Mod Podge to put the sparkle back in.

● **Water color**

Many people model water as a bright blue color. This may be the case in many instances, but the U.K., where I live, is often surrounded by a more gray colored sea, our canals are mud colored, and are rivers are certainly not blue.

Water itself is normally clear but may have muddy or green tones from soil or algae in suspension. The blue color commonly associated with water comes from the water absorbing the red spectrum of light, leaving the blue for us to see. Sunny days will have brighter blues in the sea than cloudy days, for example.

Water is also a great mirror. We have all seen photos of mountains reflected perfectly in calm lakes. This means that the color we perceive in the water is also a reflection, mostly of the sky and surrounding scenery. This makes matching it very difficult, but we can ensure that our view points allow for the scenery we model to reflect in our water if appropriate.

With clear deep water, the depth may also have an impact. Muddy, shallow, or choppy water that is fairly opaque will show little variety in color across the whole water area, whereas clear deep water will start lighter toward the edges and darken as it becomes deeper and the underlying surface shows through less. With shallow banks, this can become obvious, but with steeper water edges, it has less of an impact. This effect is particularly noticeable from above, the angle we often see model water.

Water will also impact the surrounding scenery. A coast line is the obvious place to see this as the tidal range changes twice daily and the rocks will often be damp and therefore darker where the tide has receded. Likewise, locks will also show damp walls if the water has recently been lowered. The splash area around a weir or waterfall or the rocks surrounding a river may be damp and green as they regularly remain moist. Regular floods may change the colors at the water's edge and this is often most noticeable on manmade structures, such as bridge abutments or docks.

Color therefore becomes key in modeling water correctly, and good photos of the water and the surrounding area in the conditions that you are modeling will be invaluable.

WATER FEATURES

● Puddles and small pools

These can be added anywhere, even where there is no water body. Good examples are in barrels, hollows or junk piles, but also at the bottom of ditches, road ruts and potholes, or boggy areas. The key to selling these is not just a gloss shine, but also darker colors in the damp or wet patches.

There are many acrylic products, such as AK Interactive Still Water, that you can just drip into place. These products will self-level and add a thick gloss layer over the existing scenery layer. You will need to spread the edges to avoid a domed edge, and I find they go best over a fully dried base as they can crack as they set otherwise.

You can also use gloss varnishes, but varnishes are best not poured on thickly as it is not their intended use and they may dry unevenly or crack and ripple. Solvent varnishes often yellow over time, so I tend to stick to acrylic products as a result. Tamiya Clear Coat is one of my favorite varnishes for small puddles or glossy mud effects as it is relatively thick and high gloss.

For puddles and small pools, I have started to use UV setting resin as it is easy to drip in place, then cure with a UV light. The main advantage is that it does not shrink as it dries, unlike most acrylic products.

The key with puddles is to not use any of these products in too thick layers as they are generally designed for thin applications.

CHOICES There are many products you can use to make puddles. These are three of them, from left, acrylic water product (AK Interactive Still Water), UV curing resin, and Wilder Murky Water by NitroLine, which is an enamel for scale models, but gives a beautiful gloss effect.

Resin is the most suited to deep puddles as it does not shrink and the UV resin is very easy to use as it sets in a minute through a reaction to UV light. This enables very quick modeling of puddles without waiting for anything to dry.
The enamel product, Murky Water, spreads through surrounding scenery to give a great coloration. I would recommend combining this with a resin if you want deep puddles.

OIL SLICKS are surprisingly hard to model. Here I used iridescent inks and clear paints to add colors to a resin pool. The trick is to find an ink with fine enough particles to look good in scale. I used Daler Rowney shimmering blue ink after trying many brands, and now I would also try color shift paints which are very thin in consistency and can have a number of colors depending on the viewing angle.

ADDING RIPPLES My dock water has a painted black base with a couple layers of colored resin over the top. I had not finished working on my car float and tug when I did the water ripples on my dock, and I wanted the boats to be removable. I wrapped them in cling film, then used acrylic gloss medium applied with a palette knife to create the waves. There is an area of slightly flatter water next to the tug where it has turned and the turbulence disrupts the normal wave pattern. If any of the cling film gets stuck in the gloss medium when it is dry then it can be trimmed and left in place and because it is clear, it does not show.

The water itself can be achieved with a wide variety of gloss products, many of which are probably already in your stock. Gloss varnish or Mod Podge, PVA glue, or a specialist water product can all be used. You will probably need at least a couple of coats. This technique never gives any depth to the actual water, so the gloss is to represent the shine of the water. You can then add ripples or waves per the techniques in that section.

● Ripples and waves

Water is rarely dead calm, so modeling ripples and waves can help improve the realism. Whatever the base layer, whether it be resin or a flat, smooth gloss base, you will normally need to add ripples and sometimes larger waves.

There are so many products to model ripples and small waves, but my two favorites are gloss Mod Podge for small ripples and hybrid polymer for larger textures. The hybrid polymer brand I use is ClearFix by Everbuild. It is similar to a silicone sealant, but is easily thinned and paint sticks to it. I use it in the Weirs and Waterfalls step by step.

Until recently I always used acrylic gloss mediums. These can be bought as artists products or specialist modeling products. They all have a similar make up—an acrylic gloss gel that can be spread on the water surface and manipulated to give ripples. Over the years, I have tried many of them and the key features are that they are thick enough to hold the shape, that they dry clear relatively quickly, and that they do not rewet if you need to work on the scenery around them.

To achieve the wave texture, you can use a wide range of implements from art brushes to palette knives. Experimenting with pushing the gel using a fan shaped brush or using suction from pulling up a flat palette knife will give a wide range of effects and produce many different types of wave. Another popular method is to use an airbrush or straw to blow the gel into waves which can be very effective, especially over large areas. A key issue to look out for is adding bubbles into your waves in the way you add texture. These can dry in place and ruin the look.

Some water methods will naturally give ripples, such as using a textured water sheet. You can purchase commercial lake or ripple effect materials, then cut them to size. The material has a ripple texture molded in. I have seen modelers use household obscured acrylic vanity panels to model lakes successfully. These can be painted on the under side to give a realistic water color.

● Larger flat water bodies

Water bodies are generally flat, so these techniques will cover everything from lakes to the sea, a large river or canal, or even the water in an open water tower. These are the simplest types of water to model and can be as simple as a piece of painted, flat (level) sheet material (preferably with no texture) before adding a gloss layer and ripples. The flat area needs to be planned from the beginning to ensure the water surface is below the surrounding scenery and completely level.

I prefer not to use plywood as the wood texture will show through even after a few layers of gloss coat. I therefore tend to use MDF, styrene, foam core, or card for the base. However, some cardstock can warp when using water-based products if not properly glued down and sealed.

For large areas of water, I mix up a batch of paint sufficient for two coats, mostly craft acrylics, although I have used emulsion or latex paint for larger areas. This paint needs to be the color of the deepest water. For shallow edged water, you will need to blend it to the edge earth color. Areas of deeper water should be painted a darker color.

Resin water can be prodded into wave shapes before it fully sets. This is a bit of trial and error. You will need to test regularly to catch the resin as it is setting between the semi liquid stage where it self levels again, but before the set stage where it cannot be manipulated. It is very effective, though, when successful. I have seen stunning waves achieved by grinding resin to shape after it has cured, but this is both time-consuming and messy compared to other methods.

Larger waves can be modeled using the gloss mediums, but they will take a long time to dry fully clear if applied too thickly. Some of my first sea areas took several months or longer. If these are white-crested then it may not be an issue, but I have found it to look less than realistic, and patience is not my strong suit. The clear result can be an issue if the waves are too large as the coloring may start to lose some of the variety needed to convey realism.

For larger waves therefore, it can be beneficial to model the waves in the underlying scenery layer using plaster, Sculptamold, foam, thick foil, or even toilet paper. Once the waves are modeled, they can be painted in suitable colors and a gloss layer applied. These have the advantage of modeling the waves in a relatively easy sculpting material and the final paint can capture the nuances of waves.

White water is easily represented with white paint, as I demonstrate on the resin river step by step, but there are also some other methods that can be very effective. Snow products, such as Woodland Scenics snow, can be used to add the froth to the top of waves. This can be mixed in with resin or gloss medium and the additional volume, texture and color give a realistic white water effect as in the weir step by step. Other similar powders can be used, such as micro balloons, and even small glass balls. There are also products that add a translucent white color which gives a more subtle effect than a stark white paint.

For extreme waves, you can add in cotton wool or polyfiber to add more structure and height. These are usually coated in resin or gloss medium. When that dries, the white color of the cotton or polyfiber shows through and gives a feeling of depth to the water. You can also use these without a gloss coat to represent the spray at the bottom of waterfalls.

FROTH When the first layer of gloss medium was dry, I also added a lot of froth to the stern to represent the hard work the tug has been undertaking to push the car float into place. This also masks an area where my resin did not set properly and the additional layer of acrylic gloss medium sealed in the area effectively.

STEP BY STEP • FLAT WATER AND SIMPLE RIPPLES

1 This sea dock inlet is made on a base of card, painted with craft acrylics, then covered with a layer of PVA (white) glue. The ripples were made with a thicker PVA glue streaked on. This is a very cheap and easy way to make water with small waves.

2 This is a small coastal inlet, but with a lock between it and the sea so it is not tidal at this point. The water has a distinctly greenish muddy hue, and will be much duller in the final layout as I visited on a sunny day but the layout is set on a drizzly overcast day.

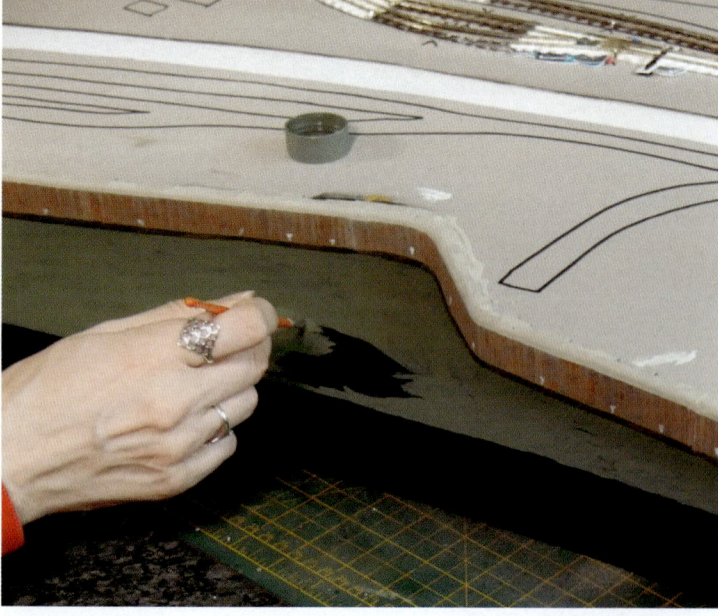

3 Preparation is key to this water effect. I started with a layer of flat gray card, as in the unfinished scenery behind. I then used a black masonry paint to seal it and also paint the fascia at the same time. Finally, I needed to color the water itself. I looked at a lot of photos from duller days and chose a greenish tone shown here I painted using an acrylic model paint.

4 The water itself is all made from PVA glue to demonstrate that water does not have to be made from hard-to-buy or expensive materials. You will need to experiment to ensure your PVA dries clear as many have a slight chalky tone. You can now buy clear PVA glues which will always dry clear.

5 When dry, you can see the brush strokes slightly, but this would pass as an area of dead calm water.

6 I added ripples using PVA tacky glue. It is slightly thicker than the first glue I used, so it stays in the ripple shapes without spreading. I used the nozzle to form the ripples, but a cocktail stick run through afterward can help make a finer ripple.

7 The ripples did look a little too stark, so I finished with a top coat of the first, thinner PVA. This did turn all my ripples bright white again but they dried clear.

8 You can build up multiple layers to get deeper ripples if you need them, but I found one layer was sufficient for the sheltered body of water I was modeling.

STEP BY STEP • RIPPLES

1 Ripples can be made from a wide variety of readily available artists materials as well as commercial modeling products. Ripples do not require specialist tools. These methods use a straw, airbrush, paint brushes, and a palette knife.

All the methods start with applying a thin layer of the ripple product to the water layer. I demonstrate four application methods but you can mix and match and use other commercial products to achieve a variety of results.

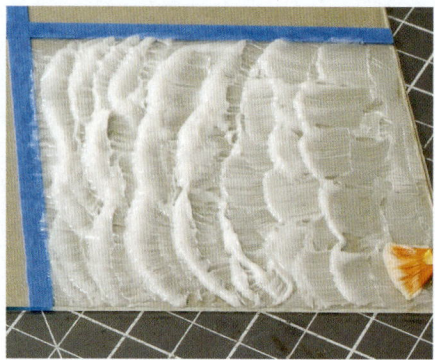

2 Method 1: acrylic gloss medium and a brush.
Acrylic gloss medium is a white gel that dries clear. It holds the waves particularly well, but can take a while to dry.

I use a fan-shaped brush to push the gloss medium into wave shapes, then pull away to create the smoother back of the wave. This works well for seas and bodies of water with larger waves. Different brushes create different wave patterns, and a smaller fan brush will give smaller waves. For rivers, I brush the ripples on with a round brush using photos as a guide (see the resin river step-by-step).

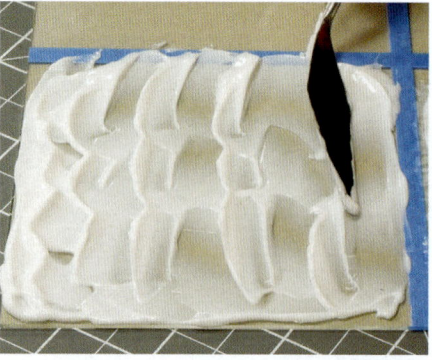

3 Method 2: acrylic gloss medium and a palette knife.
Large areas can be covered using a palette knife as I used for the dock water on my layout.

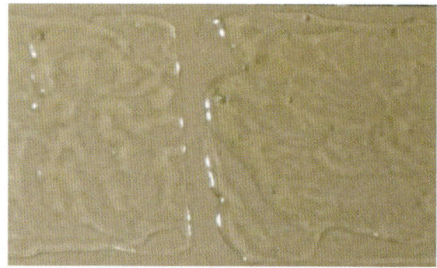

4 Method 3: gloss Mod Podge and a straw.
Gloss Mod Podge is slightly thinner than the acrylic gloss mediums, which makes it ideal for methods which use blowing. It also includes a resin so it dries to a slightly tougher finish.

In this method I used a straw to blow the Mod Podge into ripples. It works well in small areas and is very cheap to do.

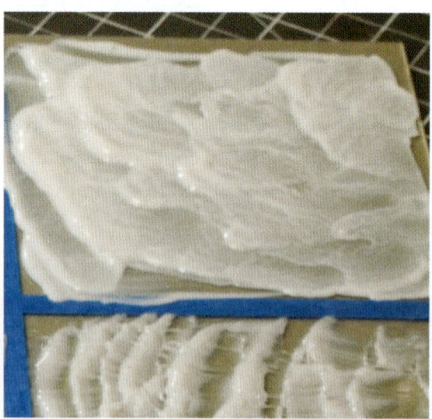

5 Method 4: gloss Mod Podge and an airbrush.
For larger areas, an airbrush (without paint!) is easier to use than a straw. You will need to practice to achieve a nice rippled effect but the final result is very natural.

6 The real difference between the two products used here is the drying time. The gloss Mod Podge, top photo, dried clear in under a day, but the acrylic gloss medium was still not clear by two days and longer (bottom photo), although it did finally dry almost clear. On the larger waves, the outer layer dries and slows the middle from drying completely. I would not recommend thick applications without testing your product's time to fully clear first.

Recently, I have started to use a hybrid polymer instead of acrylic gloss medium for larger waves. It is already clear and dries within 24 hours. However, it is a little stickier to use.

Thinner gels, such as the gloss Mod Podge, work best for river ripples where the waves are less pronounced.

FOIL AND GLUE This technique uses scrunched up foil covered with sheets of foil and works well for larger waves, especially when modeling coastal areas. A thick layer of white glue primes the foil so it can be easily painted. The foam and spray techniques are the same as the waterfalls step by step.

SPACKLE WAVES These stunning On30 waves were modeled by Troels Kirk using Polyfilla Elastic (also called flexible) spackle compound for the larger waves. He forms these by squeezing out a line of spackle, then using a dry finger to draw back the wave. He then steepens the front of the wave with a wet finger. He also used a sculpting tool to add further detail. He then paints realistic white and gray water followed up with smaller acrylic gloss gel wavelets to add more sparkle to the area. Troels used a palette knife or finger pulled upward to give these gel wavelets texture. The colors used are realistic and fit with Troels' subdued color palette across his layout. *Troels Kirk*

TOILET PAPER The unusual ingredient used to model these waves is toilet paper. Martin Tärnrot adds three layers of toilet paper, each thoroughly soaked with a wood glue and water mix. He uses a large paint brush to dab out any patterns or lines where the layers mix. Finally, he uses the brush to push waves into the toilet paper layers. Once dry, he paints the waves with artists acrylics blended with darker colors to the center to represent deeper water. *Martin Tärnrot*

PRODDED RESIN These waves were made by prodding the resin as it set. It took several attempts because if you do it too early, the resin levels back out, but if you leave it too late, the resin cannot be pushed well. I tested every half hour until I hit the right time. This also shows a common problem with water—dust—or in this case, snow. The fine snow is very hard to clear off the resin as it falls back on again. This resin is very scratch-resistant but large water bodies will need regular dusting to remain looking good.

● Streams and shallow rivers

Streams and shallow rivers can be modeled using the flat water or puddle techniques already discussed, but I prefer to use materials that allow more depth to show. This means that the banks and river or stream bottoms can show through, as well any embedded debris or lock machinery.

The best products for adding deeper water are those that rely on a chemical reaction to set, such as resins. They do not shrink like water-based products, which is vital in deeper layers, and they always self-level so the water surface is flat. Added to that, they are relatively easy to use to achieve realistic deep water results.

Resin is the best known deep water product and is a two part product. It can be tinted with paints, although adding a lot of a water-based paint can result in foaming in some types of resin, especially epoxy resins. You can buy ready-colored resins from many manufacturers, removing that worry about using tints, specifically aimed at scale models. I find that resins like Envirotex Lite, a common choice, are slightly brown and darken over time. This suits my colored water, but it is something to bear in mind.

The chemical reaction generates heat and the deeper the pour, the hotter it can get. Resins that cure more quickly generally have a hotter curing temperature and, conversely, longer curing times and shallower pours will be cooler. When choosing a base, ensure that the base is able to cope with the generated heat and be careful of any plastic details in the resin. These can and do melt. A foam base may also be affected by the heat.

Resin will often trap bubbles that can be removed by running a heat source quickly over the surface, such as a heat gun or blow torch. Blowing can also work as the heat in the breath pops the bubbles. You may need to come back over several hours to remove them all.

One consideration with resin is that it is a very thin liquid that will happily spread through your surrounding scenery, finding the lowest point and any holes. I certainly have had more than a few leaks in my time, some through the base but most at the ends where my attempts at dams had not worked quite well enough. I regularly see people using something like masking tape successfully, but mine just peeled off and the resin flooded out. Now I use acetate strips, glued on with hot glue or silicon glue. If I use a different glue then I also seal around the edges with some additional white glue.

Leaks are easily avoided by ensuring the ends of a water

The railroad runs along a shallow river on Tom Harris' Lakeside Lines. Resin is the best choice for modeling the muddy color and visible rocky bed.
Tom Harris

course are well dammed and that the base layers are thick enough to avoid any holes. A product like Woodland Scenics Shaper Sheet is also good as the foil is leakproof but easily formed into realistic contours.

Resin gives a modeler the opportunity to add a plethora of details, from riverbed rocks, fallen branches, and water plants to swimming people. These all need to be planned before the river is started to ensure you embed them in the resin. Resin can also be colored and poured in layers so that a thin bottom layer can be darker or muddier and the top layers can be relatively clear allowing a great feeling of depth in a relatively flat model.

Clear encapsulation silicone rubber is a two part mix like a resin and can be used instead. It has some advantages, such as no bubbles, no fumes, and no heat, but it can be a little water repellent meaning some ripple products do not work as well. I used a solvent glue nearby and did not wait long enough for the solvents to evaporate and it did inhibit the rubber from setting. However, I have found it to be another useful product in the arsenal.

STEP BY STEP • RESIN RIVER

● There are a wide range of resin products that can be used for water, some specifically aimed at the model railroad market and many from the wider modeling manufacturers. Nowadays, you can even buy pre-colored resins that can be used to represent murky water. I like Magic Water as it is slightly rubbery and easy to trim back. Some resins are equal parts mix, and some have a different ratio, either by weight or volume. Do make sure to read the instructions well before mixing.

SMALL SCENES Resin does not just have to be used for large streams and rivers. It gives a great gloss shine when applied over normal ground layers. This can be used in boggy areas or areas where water is trickling rather than a proper stream as in this small culvert area. Acrylic gloss medium can be used to add ripples if desired.

BUILDING A RESIN STREAM These two views of a resin stream show how the layers are built up with the foundation layer, earth and stones, resin, acrylic gloss ripples, and white froth all visible.

STEP BY STEP • RESIN RIVER

1 This type of river needs a highly detailed base. For this diorama, I used Sculptamold as the foundation layer followed by Woodland Scenics talus, starting with extra coarse and moving through to fine. The talus is excellent for rivers as it has a rounded shape. I pushed the larger stones into the still wet Sculptamold so they were bedded into the ground rather than sitting on top of it.

2 Once the Sculptamold was dry, I added tile grout to fill any remaining gaps. I put it in place with a brush, then wiped any rocks clear before spraying with the normal two step scenery glue method of dilute isopropyl alcohol followed by dilute matte Mod Podge. This also helped glue down some of the smaller talus stones that were a little loose.

3 I painted these rocks a gray color and added some yellow greens to represent lichen. To add a feeling of depth, I dripped on a black acrylic wash. This sinks in around the rocks and highlights the surface texture of the talus as well. You must wait for your scenery to fully dry before moving on to pouring any resin.

4 Good dams are crucial to successful resin rivers. I use sheet acrylic and glued it in place with white glue. I have used silicon and hot glue in the past, but whatever glue used, it needs to be easy to remove afterward. The glue also needs to be a thin layer to avoid the river protruding in front of the layout edge. It goes without saying but do ensure your dam is tall enough and that the glue goes up the sides too or the resin will leak.

5 Resins are two-part and rely on a chemical reaction to set. This is different than acrylic products, which dry to set. This resin is Magic Water, but there are loads of different commercial resins you can use. As you can see, this is quite old and although it still sets, one part of it has turned brown. Resins often color with time, leaving a browner shade than perhaps wanted. Research your brand of resin well before committing to a large area. This is a 2:1 mix so I weigh the resin on a scale to ensure an accurate ratio. If you do have problems with your resin setting because of inadequate measuring or mixing, then just pour another layer on top or add a thick ripple layer. I have done this successfully more than once and with the ripples in place, no one will notice.

6 Resin needs to be stirred well but not so vigorously that loads of small bubble are introduced. Because this was already brown, I did not add any paint, but I would normally color at least the first pour of a river with an appropriate color paint. You can now buy pre-colored resin with shades such as murky.

Some resins do react very badly to water so, while I use acrylic paints to color mine, it is best to do so in a test piece first rather than on your final product. The types of resin that react with water can foam up badly, ruining your scenery, so it is also important to make sure that your scenery is fully dry before adding the resin.

7 I pour down a stick until the river is full. Resin will not shrink, but some resins can get very hot. Deep pours will exacerbate this, to the extent that they can melt a foam base underneath. This can be avoided by either pouring multiple thin layers, which enables you to build up darker colors at the bottom getting lighter in the top layers, or by making sure that the Sculptamold is sufficiently thick to insulate. Magic Water does not heat up, but the corollary can be that the resin takes longer to cure.

Resin typically has a lot of bubbles in it when poured. Some brands are worse than others. I use Magic Water because it has hardly any bubbles, but you will need to burst any you do have to ensure a clear river. The bubbles float to the top and are easy to pop by waving a chef's blow torch or similar over the resin. You can also breathe on them to pop them, but it is not as effective. Finally, cover your water with a sheet of paper and put it somewhere warm to set. Heat will hasten the curing process.

STEP BY STEP • RESIN RIVER

8 Once the resin is set and has lost the squeaky feeling when you rub it, you can start adding reeds and vegetation around the edges. Some resins creep a lot into the surrounding earth layer and you can add more of that layer over the edge of the resin to mask this. As you can see, after the resin was cured, I added the rest of the scenery. I cover the resin when spraying glue to avoid the surface becoming dull, and I ensure I clean off any scenery materials that do fall on it as soon as possible.

9 When the dam is removed, there is often a meniscus, a raised rim. This can be trimmed off with a sharp knife. The next steps will mask this.

10 This is a white river and needed waves to show this. I used artists acrylic gloss gel and used a brush to push the gel into wave shapes, following my prototype photo as a guide. The gel also needs to cover where we trimmed the raised edge at the dam.

11 The acrylic gel goes on white but dries clear, so I used a white paint to add back the froth at the top of the waves. I used a matte paint so I needed to go over it with another layer of gloss. I used gloss Mod Podge, to add the shine back.

● Moving water

Moving water adds so much life to a scene whether it be a mill canal weir, a fast running stream or even an effluent pipe gushing out dirty water.

Before you start building the scenery, you will need to plan a change in height to allow the water to drop realistically. This can be as simple as a small weir or rapids all the way through to a spectacular long drop waterfall.

Waterfalls are a three-step process starting with a clear base, such as acetate or acrylic sheet, cut to shape. A clear gloss product, much the same as for ripples, is used to build up the texture. The final step is to add some white water froth at the bottom.

The main products used are:

- Acrylic gloss gels, as used for ripples, can be used but when added too thickly, the time taken to dry clear can become a real issue.
- Silicone sealant or glue was the first product I used on waterfalls and it remains one of my favorites as it starts clear and dries clear without shrinking. The only pitfall is that it is water repellent, so adding paint to represent froth can result in it beading. This effect can look realistic and I also like to run my final resin pour down the waterfall to add further color and to bed it in.
- Hybrid polymer sealants are a newer version of silicone sealants and do not have the same issues with repelling the resin, making them easier to use. In addition, they can be thinned with more readily available solvents, such as white spirit.

SLOWING FAST WATER These culverts are some of my earliest modeling. The left hand photograph shows my actual model and the water is gloss medium over acetate. The acetate is straight and, while water may flow out at great force in a straighter line, it will fall in an arc. I used the magic of Photoshop to show a much more realistic shape for this kind of flow.

EXPECT LEAKS Despite my best efforts, the resin in this river leaked when I poured it. Thankfully I had covered the lower level with some plastic bags and foam core. Another top tip: keep the mixing cup so you can tell when your resin is cured without having to touch your model and risk leaving fingerprints.

TALL FALLS Howard Zane modeled waterfalls on his layout using clear silicone caulk textured with a wide-tooth comb or plastic fork with highlights in white paint. *Forrest Nace*

STEP BY STEP • WEIRS AND WATERFALLS

There are so many different products that can be used to make waterfalls, but the techniques are very similar in most cases. The effluent pipe photo further on shows the same technique using resin water and silicone sealant for the falls.

This step by step will work whether you choose to model a river using resin or another deep-pour product or just to use sheets of flat water. The top and bottom are easily blended in with ripple products in the latter case.

1 Prepare your base as for a river with a painted base and rocks. I also added a wash of green paint across rocks and especially toward the bottom where they meet the river.

2 The weirs or waterfalls can be made from any gel product that dries clear and is flexible. I chose the hybrid polymer ClearFix here, but crystal clear silicone sealant or an acrylic gloss medium will work.

Spread the product onto a clear plastic bag or acetate sheet and spread it into the right shape for the waterfall. Add vertical streaks with a stirrer or cocktail stick. Smooth the top into a rounded shape and tail it out to provide the start of the waterfall on the upper level. This needs to be as thin as possible so it can be bent, but also blended in with the ripples if a flat water technique rather than a poured resin is used for the main river.

3 You do not have to bed the waterfall into a resin or rubber river but it will help hide the top and bottom fixing points if you do.

If you are using resin, remember to dam any areas where the river could run out. You will also need to ensure that the concrete dam or rock for the waterfall itself is high enough to hold the upper level river. The waterfall will need to fill the whole width of the dam or the resin will flow around the edges.

4 The waterfall should peel off the base, but if it does not, cut around the waterfall. Using a clear bag or sheet means if it is still attached, it will not show.

5 Paint white streaks on the back of the waterfall leaving some clear areas still.

6 Trim the waterfall to size and test fit in place.

7 I used ClearFix to attach the river to the top and bottom because it dries clear, but you can also use any of the products you used to create your waterfall.

8 Bend the top of the waterfall over the edge of the dam or rockface where the waterfall starts. If you are just using a flat sheet for the water, the top of the waterfall should be glued down against this as it is thin enough to do so.

Do consider whether the upper level water is sufficiently dammed to allow it to cover the top of the waterfall when poured and add a little more of the waterfall product if needed to fill any gaps to the sides.

STEP BY STEP • WEIRS AND WATERFALLS

9 I love using Woodland Scenics snow to make the froth and foam that need to be modeled. I mix the hybrid polymer and the snow together, adding enough mineral spirits to keep the mixture workable. This can be thin or thick depending on how much froth you want. This step can also be done with acrylic gloss medium and thinned with water if needed.

10 I spread this mixture thinly over the waterfall to add bubbles and froth to it. I then build up the bottom froth of the waterfall. If you are using flat water beds and not pouring resin then you can skip to step 17 and carry on with the finer froth and foam.

11 I used rubber glass, a Smooth-on product, for my river. This is an excellent alternative to epoxy resin for those that are allergic to it. It does have a couple of quirks, one being that the waterfall products I used inhibited the cure as I did not allow sufficiently long for the solvents in them to dissipate. I did some tests and leaving the froth and foam a week before pouring was sufficient to allow the rubber to set properly. The second quirk is that thinner acrylic gloss mediums, such as gloss Mod Podge, will not spread on the surface, meaning that solvent-based products or thicker gels need to be used to make the ripples.

Like epoxy resin, it is a two-part mix. The main advantage is that it does not hold bubbles so it dries completely bubble free. I colored it with silicone pigments using a spot of white to add some opacity.

12 Start pouring on the upper level to ensure you reach the level of your waterfall.

13 Remember to pour some water over the falls to slightly color the white to match the water and to add some shine.

14 I used a cotton bud to swab the river product all around the waterfall where spray or dampness would accumulate.

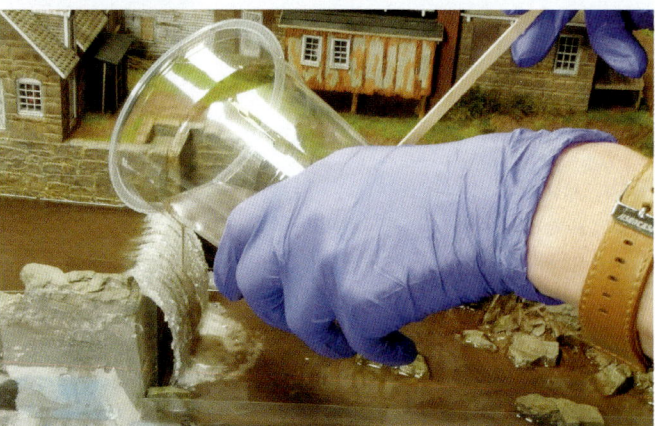

15 I did two pours with a day in between to get the desired depth I wanted. The bottom foam is still visible through the water, giving great depth to the effect. Once it is set, I remove the dams.

16 You can use the same froth material to add another layer where it would naturally occur. I recommend using photos as an aid for placement.

17 I thinned the mix down with more mineral spirits and added another layer of much finer foam to represent the waves and bubbles.

18 For even finer foam, I use white acrylic paint dabbed on with a brush.

19 Finally, I built up the ripples using thinned ClearFix and a brush for the texture. This layer is clear and adds the smaller ripple textures.

● **Special techniques**

WHICH PRODUCT?
There are so many products available now that it can be hard to work out which one to use. They fall into three main categories:
- **Acrylic products**—these are one-part liquids that set by drying; as a result, they will normally shrink a little as they dry. They are not suitable for deep pours, but work well for adding flat glossy areas.
- **Resin products**—these are two-part and work best to represent deep water where the river bed or other items need to be visible beneath the surface. They will need waves added in most circumstances, so should be used in conjunction with acrylic ripple products. I have recently tried crystal-clear encapsulation rubber, which works similarly to resin but does not generate heat or fumes.
- **Ripple products**—these are generally acrylic based and often are white but clear as they dry.

EFFLUENT PIPE Pipes, overflows and drains are all opportunities to add water details to our layouts. This effluent pipe was made using colored resin over an acetate strip. The colored resin was continued into the river resin while both were still uncured so it looks like the effluent is being carried away downstream. The weir was made using resin and silicone as per the step by step for waterfalls.

A QUICK SHINE The ClearFix used in the weirs and waterfalls step by step does dry slightly matte, so I added Tamiya Clear to give it a nice robust gloss finish.

BOGGY AREA Bogs and damp patches are easy to add to any low-lying areas of a layout and can make a small feature. This bog was modeled using a 2-part resin with commercial grass clumps used as reeds. Ground foam added more texture to the water surface.

Lou Sassi

CHAPTER ELEVEN

Buildings in scenery

Model buildings and structures are a huge subject and one chapter will not do them justice. Instead, we will concentrate on the scenery aspects of buildings and how to ensure they fit within your layout. Buildings appear on all layouts, whether they be urban or rural. They are usually the most obvious item in a scene, after the railroad, and our eye is often drawn to them. This gives us an opportunity to show off our modeling and learn new skills. Structures, such as a coaling tower or car float bridge, also signpost an area's purpose and give great opportunities for modeling.

Whether it is a big city or a humble outhouse, buildings are an aspect of scenery that we all need to master. Howard Clark's railroad is the epitome for many of a city scene with trains running through urban canyons past highly detailed and weathered buildings.

URBAN MODELING Rensselaer Model Railroad Club captured a perfect street-running scene on its Berkshire Lines. The layout's city of Troy features 20 city blocks of scratchbuilt and kitbashed structures. This view looks along the model railroad and shows well-weathered buildings, interesting street running, and a mix of road surfaces. All these elements add up to realistic urban modeling.

Street running brings its own challenges as the track work becomes buried. It does need to be running perfectly before this as any bugs are impossible to fix easily afterward. *Lou Sassi*

INSPIRING MODELING George Sellios' Franklin & South Manchester is probably the best-known urban layout. He has incorporated two cities in his layout as well as smaller towns. His use of height, sprawling urban buildings, and stunning scenery remain an inspiration to countless modelers. *Richard Josselyn*

● Buildings and structures

Signature buildings or structures can help set the location, such as an adobe hut for the Southwest, a grain silo for the Midwest, or a New England mill. Not only can these structures set the scene, they can also interact with the railroad, such as a grain silo or mill acting as an area of operations. This interaction means such buildings and structures need to be planned from the earliest stages.

While planning my layout, I cut out the footprints of all the major buildings, often craftsman kits yet to be built, and I used them to ensure clearances, siding locations, scenic contours, and view blocks. For some areas, I photocopied photos onto card and built mockups. This is most useful when a view block is needed or in urban scenes where the skyline is important. I glued a lot of my plastic structure kits together so I could put them in place and come back and paint them later on. This enabled me to think and plan in 3D. Today, I might use a 3D design program to mock up the rough shapes to see how they fit together. I also consider road and rail access to the buildings to add more scenic elements.

Many manufacturers supply footprints in the product details, and I often used these to work out which building kits to buy to fit into certain locations. Modular buildings have opened up new opportunities for creating custom structures. For awkward spots or unique structures, it may be necessary to scratchbuild. Regardless of whether you love scratchbuilding or kitbashing, prefer to build out-of-the-box kits, or buy ready-built buildings, they all need to fit into your scenery.

● Urban modeling

Cities and towns bring their own challenges as we try to fit large structures into our relatively small spaces. Sight lines, view blocks, and forced perspective were all looked at in the planning chapter and are techniques that can help our real estate seem larger.

With size a key issue, selective

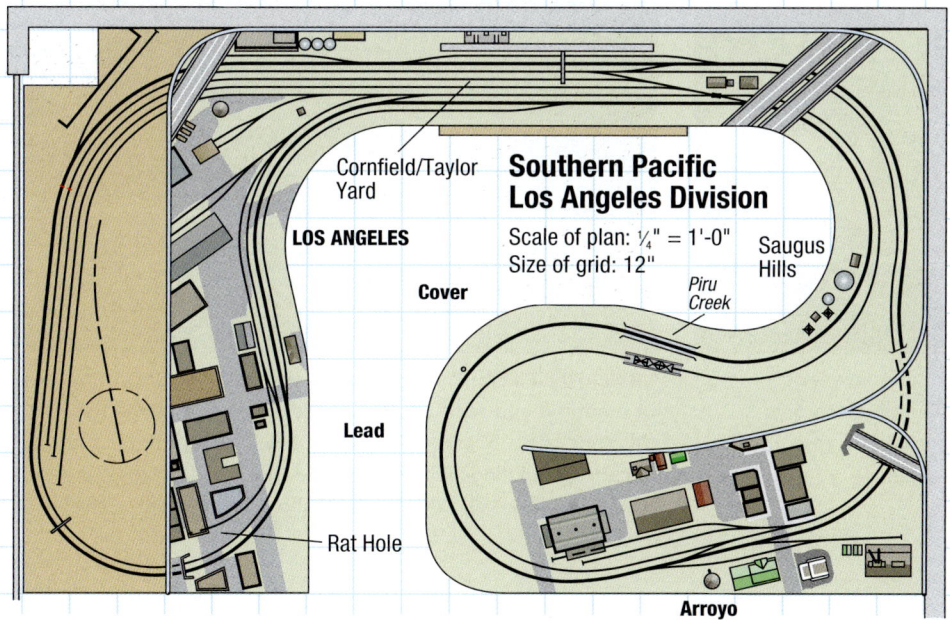

STRATEGIC PLACEMENT

Robert Smaus captured a slice of Los Angeles in 3 x 12 feet in the Alameda Street and Rat Hole part of his Southern Pacific Los Angeles Division layout. He featured key scenes from the area such as the Rat Hole, which features a curved building adjacent to the track. The section also features narrow alleys, which hint at a much larger area than is actually visible. One key technique that Robert uses is to ensure his buildings hit the backdrop at an angle so a viewer standing straight on does not look up the streets to a blank wall. The use of T-junctions and corners plus low relief back buildings all help give the illusion of endless city.
Robert Smaus

compression is a common technique that can help and simply means that a structure is built as shorter or narrower than the original. Where a grain elevator may have eight silos in the prototype, the model may only have six. This can give the full flavor of the building in three quarters of the space, for example. Many model kits are already compressed with this in mind.

However, when it comes to cities, reaching upward with extra stories to buildings can also add to the city feel. This extra height reflects the view that we have standing at the edge of a tall building; we can see nothing behind it and it fills our field of view.

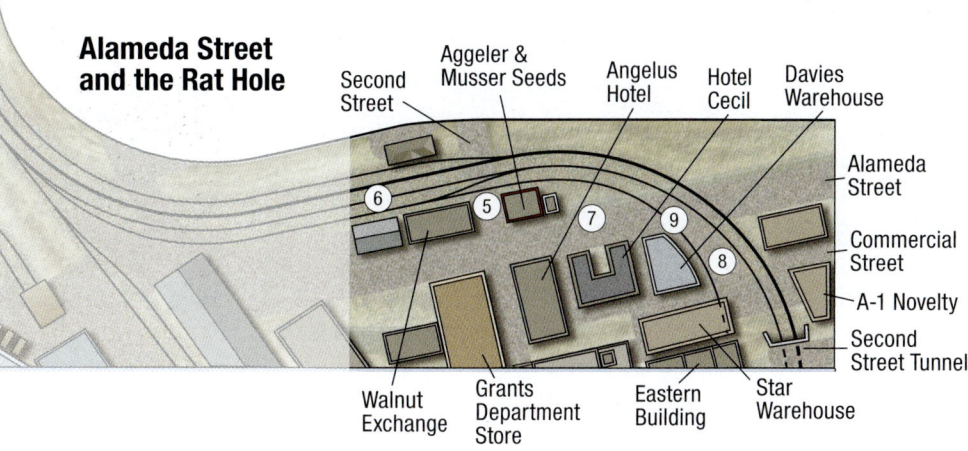

● Maritime and industrial modeling

Large industries and ports are often focal points on a layout, indeed some are layouts in their own right. These are probably the most selectively compressed models as their footprints are too large for the average layout. However, capturing the essence of these structures is enough to allow a viewer to believe that they are looking at a realistic scene.

LAND AND SEA There is something appealing about the mix of maritime and rail. Cliff Powers captures that perfectly with this shot of his Mississippi, Alabama & Gulf layout. He marries backdrop buildings with weathered buildings, bridges and water. Small details, such as the fisherman, add life. *Cliff Powers*

MULTIPLE LAYERS Joe Kaspar used multiple layers of buildings from his backdrop to the pier buildings to give a feeling of depth to his New York harbor layout, the Pennsylvania RR Eastern Division. *Joe Kaspar*

EXPANSIVE STRUCTURES Pelle Søeborg dedicated 12 feet of his layout to a scratchbuilt cement plant. This signature structure occupies one third of his layout and features highly detailed and weathered structures made from kit parts or built from styrene and brass parts by Pelle. *Pelle Søeborg*

EXPERIENCE ON DISPLAY Mike Rabbitt's HO scale steel industry is the focus of his layout and comes from his own working experience. *Paul J. Dolkos*

MINIMAL STRUCTURES Gary Hoover added a couple of railroad structures—relay cabinets and a signal—on an otherwise rural flatlands scene on his former HO scale Missouri, Kansas & Quincy RR. *Gary Hoover*

VISUAL BALANCE This rural scene on Trond Atle Olsen and Jon Einar Vistad's module features a small number of buildings. The buildings do not overpower the module, and there is sufficient space around them that the overall impression is one of countryside. Trond was able to take the module outside to photograph it, but a similar backdrop effect could be created with a photograph. *Trond Atle Olsen*

● Rural scenes

A chapter on buildings and structures will mostly focus on urban and industrial modeling, but rural areas feature structures too, whether that be barns or small houses. These can provide small cameos and allow forced perspective by using smaller scale buildings at the back of a scene.

● Practicalities

Structures are often easiest built on a workbench and added to a layout later. I build my larger craftsman kit structures on diorama bases of foam. I drop these into holes in the layout to be bedded in later with Scupltamold, or left removable if I want to replace them at a later date with a new building. This suits my style of working as I can do all the construction, including scenery, on my workbench, rather than in my layout room.

Others do the final scenery stage on the layout itself, which enables them to tie the building into the surrounding areas. Whichever is your preference, if you want removable dioramas, they need to be planned from the start, along with access. For example, I had to remove the roof from one of my taller buildings to fit it under my valence and into the layout.

VARYING DEPTHS Paul Boehlert used varying depths of backdrop buildings to fit as much as possible into as small a footprint as he could. It gives more interest behind an area that is seen from most viewpoints on his layout. *Paul Boehlert*

ADDING MASS Despite the trend for selective compression, Tony Koester often likes to expand his kit buildings to give a larger footprint. As he is modeling a city scene that is only viewable from the front, he is able to repurpose the back walls to give greater depth to his commercial buildings in this scene. Running his buildings right up to the front of the layout gives maximum usage of his layout space. You can also see how the building at the end of the street effectively hides the backdrop and gives the layout a much larger appearance of space than is really there. *Tony Koester*

WEATHERING

The first photo is the stock Walthers Wallschlager Motors ready-built structure. I weathered mine using just enamel washes and for fun showed it superimposed in the same setting as the original. A simple coat of a few colors of washes brings out the details, knocks back the shine of self-colored plastic buildings, and gives a very quick and easy weathered result. *Wm. K. Walthers (top)*

● Realistic buildings

I love scenery because it is very forgiving of mistakes, but structures need a little more precision to look real. Even basic kit buildings can be improved with a few simple features such as weathering, details, and attention to scale.

The biggest giveaway that a building is a model is the scale of details. It is very hard to model scale window mullions as they become impossibly small. However, with a careful paint scheme, you can minimise overscale details by painting them in darker colors or swap them for finer detail parts. With the advent of 3D printers, upgrading details is becoming easier.

Weathering is key to any item of scenery, but especially structures that are outside in the elements. Even relatively new buildings will show dust splashes at the base and streaks; older buildings may have moss, worn areas, rust patches and pronounced weathering.

The first stage of weathering starts with choosing the paint colors. More muted colors will give a feeling of age compared to bright colors. To tone down a building, you can fade the paint with a light airbrushing of a dust color.

I use enamel washes or dilute oil paints to weather mortar or add green algae. Pigments and pastels can be used to add dust or rust effects. I use tile grout for my earth layer, and this can be used like a pigment on the lower parts of the building where it is next to exposed ground. This will tie your buildings into that ground effectively. I use dark pink pastels to fade red oxide painted structures. The pastel chalks can be scraped with a knife blade to produce a fine powder. I mix pigments with isopropyl alcohol for a chalky wash. There are also liquid pigments available that will achieve the same effect.

You can fix weathering pigments with specialist fixers or a light spray of isopropyl alcohol, but I generally do not bother as I try not to handle my buildings and the coats are very fine. Sealing will often remove the effect, undoing most of your work and also get rid of the chalky texture.

> **DETAILS**
> Details can add an extra layer of realism to our modeling, and buildings are prime candidates. Consider adding the following:
> - Electrical meters and conduit
> - Telegraph and power poles
> - Awnings
> - Shutters and curtains
> - Weather vanes
> - Roof flashing
> - Signs
> - Fences, from wood or post and wire, to chain link and barbed wire
> - Broken windows
> - Birds and animals including bird droppings
> - People
> - Lighting, from interior lights to exterior lights and streetlights

MIND THE GAP I do have a pet peeve about buildings, passed on to me by many modelers who I really respect, and that is a black line under the building where there is a gap. It is one of the main clues that the building is a model. These gaps are easily filled with a little ground foam or earth, and it makes a huge difference. Even a small amount of dry pigment/tile grout can work for a photograph. Plasticene is another quick and easy way to fill gaps on removable buildings.

PAINT AND DETAILS Realistic weathering and painting the window mullions in a dark color has made this standard kit building look more realistic on Jim Bzdawka's HO scale layout. The building is a Walthers background structure built by Jim's son, Bill. *Jim Bzdawka*

CHAPTER TWELVE

Details

Realistic scenery consists of many layers, starting with the ground, then vegetation and structures, finally progressing through to the finer details. Details are the bits and pieces we add to a basic scene to bring it to life. These can range from signs and weathering, to animals and people.

As with all my scenery, I prefer to add more details to the front scenes of a layout where they are more visible, and to emphasise the depth of a scene by adding less to the back. This follows a typical photo where details at the front are sharp but they are less defined toward the rear. I tend to highly detail the first 6 inches and drop detail toward the back 6 inches and as my layouts are only 2 feet deep, this forces a feeling of depth.

There is a danger of adding too many details and over-cluttering a

REALISM Details like patched and cracked roads, utility poles, and fire hydrants can make a huge difference to a scene. Remove those items from this photo by Gabriel Martinez's O scale diorama and it would be quite plain and boring and far less realistic.
Jorge Martinez

TELLING A STORY Lou and Cheryl Sassi show how adding details can change a fairly plain, nondescript shed into a building with a purpose. A carpenter or workman uses this structure and the details tell a story, from the ladder to the stored wood scraps. Weeds add to the tale that this area is not used that often. *Lou Sassi*

layout. This means everything becomes a blur and it actually detracts from the realism. Not every building is a decrepit weathered ruin, not every road is cracked and worn just as not every boxcar is heavily weathered. Buildings were all new once and every road was smooth when the tarmac was newly laid. I would encourage using details to draw attention to specific details that are features, whether that be a building or a river, rather than dropping them everywhere equally.

Each of the chapters in this book already looks at specific details for those areas, so rather than list details here I will concentrate on the process.

Adding details

Details are normally the last thing added in a process, but as with most scenery, some may need to be considered from the outset if they are to be embedded in the ground. This is the fun bit of the scenery where you add people, cars and the signs of life. It is also a time to step back and look at your layout and see if any areas are over-detailed or too bare. Adjusting colors or catching any glue spots in this review can also help in selling the realism.

I love finding details, whether it is second hand at a train show, something new at a shop, or browsing through online catalogs. Over the years I have collected boxes and boxes of details and the biggest challenge is finding that one item you remember.

However, more recently I have added a new method of adding details—my resin 3D printers. These produce exquisite details with great resolution and are relatively cheap. For some specialist items, I design them myself in Blender or Fusion 360, both free software. However, I always look first to see if someone else has already done that work on websites such as Thingiverse or MyMiniFactory, which currently have loads of free products that can be scaled for my layout. I have printed people, cats, rats and dogs plus bins, oil drums and even entire buildings. For those without their own 3D printer, services such as Shapeways will print your design or have large catalogues of designs in railroad scales. The only downside is that you will need to paint the 3D printed items yourself.

3D PRINT TO THE RESCUE
Eric White designed the ornate front to this freight house as well as the roof to the skylight before having them printed at Shapeways. This is an example of a detail that makes the building really special but would be very hard to do by hand. This was his first 3D printing project and shows how accessible this technology is to the beginner. *William Zuback*

PHOTOS TO THE RESCUE V.S. Roseman shows how important details are to stop scenery looking like a model. The postman looking in a shop window is perfect for drawing the eye in. V.S. used photos from real shops and signs and printed them himself. He recommends taking photos of interiors at night if possible to cut down on reflections. Alternatively, a polarizing filter on a camera might help. *V.S. Roseman*

FIGURES DRAW US IN Scale people make a huge difference but can be easy to spot as models. Using figures in more static poses, such as looking in a shop window, sitting down, or waiting at a station platform can avoid this. Having said that, as we share our work more and more through the medium of photography, these frozen scenes become less of an issue as we are always capturing a fixed moment in time. This scene on Howard Zane's Piermont Division perfectly captures how people can be used, even in HO scale, to bring realism. *Forrest Nace*

POSE SETS THE SCENE I could not find a suitable HO scale figure for my rainy day diorama so I designed this person in MakeHuman and Blender before 3D printing and painting him. His hunched pose made all the difference to the final diorama.

DEPTH OF DETAIL I love everything about Brooks Stover's S scale scene and how it shows the importance of details. From the more detailed foreground with people and a waiting truck telling a story through to the low key clutter and railroad details such as the crossbucks. *Brooks Stover*

DECALS TO THE RESCUE Scale people can be difficult to paint with even the steadiest hand. V.S. Roseman used decals to add incredible detail to his O scale figures. *V.S. Roseman*

LIGHTING DRAWS YOU IN Perhaps one of the best-known layouts internationally and voted the most popular tourist attraction in Germany, Minatur Wunderland is known for its highly detailed moving vehicles with working lights including police cars and fire engines. Here the fire engines have been called to a fire on the side of the road. The attraction cycles through night scenes and the lights make a huge impact. Similar systems can be installed on your own layout as can adding lights to vehicles. You can even buy cars with lights pre-installed. At the very least, we should add drivers to our cars that are positioned as moving!
Erhard Baltrusch

MODEL PROJECTS JUST FOR YOU!

Item #12828 • $21.99

Do you want to take your modeling to the next level? With *Realistic Layouts* you'll learn how to blend various elements so they all work together to create a feeling that your models are part of the real world. This book features how to apply different techniques and ideas to your layout in order to improve realism and much more.

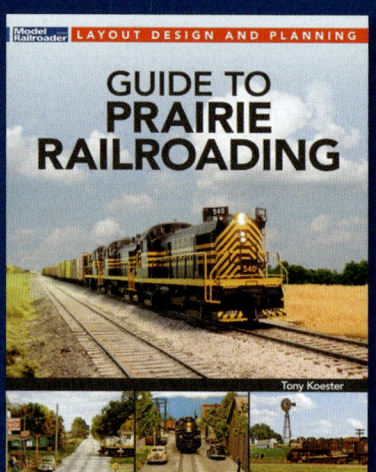

Item #12841 • $21.99

Prairie railroading has its own special appeal, and *Guide to Prairie Railroading* from Tony Koester shows you how to capture both the scenic aspects as well as prototype operations on your layout.

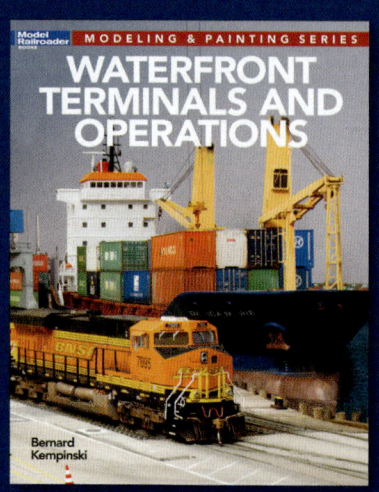

Item #12497 • $21.99

Rail-marine operations are a vital aspect of modern transportation, and *Waterfront Terminals and Operations* explores this interesting topic in model railroading. This book includes a historical overview of the railroad-marine interface - the terminal where railroad tracks meet lakes or sea, from a modeler's perspective and more.

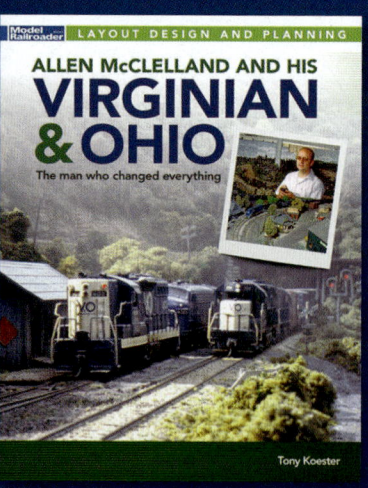

Item #12844 • $21.99

Allen McClelland made a profound impact on model railroading, and his Virginian & Ohio is one of the hobby's best-known layouts of all time. Get this historical book on the late Allen McClelland and how his influence helped bring model railroading to where it is today

Buy now from your local hobby shop or Shop at Shop.Trains.com